D1600142

PRAISE FOR *ME AND THE COTTONWOOD TREE*

"I grew up watching the stories of *The Waltons* on TV and enjoying the adventures of the Walton kids. Those stories pale in comparison to the misadventures and odd ventures of Herb's untethered boyhood. These stories make the Waltons seem like quiet, simple, boringly normal folk. Herb's grandpa could have had a sitcom just with his wacky life events. Frankly, it is a wonder Herb survived drowning in outhouses or driving lessons at 4:30 a.m. Seriously, can you even imagine a *Waltons* episode where Grandpa, in bed, gave a driving lesson at 4:30 a.m. to a twelve-year-old who was taught to drive a stick shift by holding a toilet plunger? Then expected the twelve-year-old to consistently drive six miles to do farmwork? This book is filled with crazy wisdom, like stupid places to put your thumb, the mercy of two biscuits, or things that could kill you—like riding in a child's car that is roped to the back of a Ford.

"The author—who survived all this make-you-want-to-cry-and-laugh-at-the-same-time, *Green Acres*–from-hell hazing—writes a wise, rational life-advice epilogue. The epilogue is worth the price of the book and deeply impressed this theologian. I read Herb's words, and they sound like lost pages of the Stoic philosophers Epictetus and Seneca, as well as the ideal of Epicurus, which was to enjoy the simple pleasures of life and friends."

—Rev. Dr. Paul M. Ashby

"I LOVED THE BOOK! From scorpions to swimming lessons, dances to dynamite, this is the story of a childhood well spent. Reading this book feels like you're gathered around listening to a friend tell a well-loved story, the kind that has been polished in the retelling until the ebb and flow are just right.

"Bryce's book not only opens a door into a world of boyhood mischief in the last era when it was OK to let children play with dynamite, but it also looks through that door with both feet still firmly planted in the twenty-first century. Few stories talk about World War II rationing and then go on to make a *Back to the Future* reference! Thoroughly enjoyable from cover to cover."

—Lorie Hoffman, MFA

Me and the Cottonwood Tree: An Untethered Boyhood is the delightful story of a happy childhood, full of exploration, adventure, and learning, nurtured among an expansive, multigenerational and loving family."

—Marcia Barton, English professor
emeritus, Seattle Central College

"Anyone who has a grandparent would be lucky to get a book like this. The story is not just about the shaping of one boy, it's also about a culture and way of life that is long gone. Bryce's ability to wind his family history within American history is a great gift and makes for excellent storytelling—for grandkids and the rest of us. I think I'd like to sit under that cottonwood tree myself."

—Laurie Lindblad

ME AND THE COTTONWOOD TREE

ME AND THE COTTONWOOD TREE

An Untethered Boyhood

HERB BRYCE with ANNA KATZ

HB BOOKS

Published by HB Books, Shoreline, WA
www.HerbBryce.com

Edited and designed by Girl Friday Productions
www.girlfridayproductions.com

Cover design: Anna Curtis
Project management: Bethany Davis

Image credits: cover © Anna Curtis, Image courtesy of the author
All photos courtesy of the author, except: 101, Calle Eklund; 117, Micah
Schmidt; 142, ashok india/Shutterstock; 148, Wikimedia Commons;
191, ClipArt ETC; 195, U.S. National Archives

ISBN (hardcover): 978-1-7343885-1-0
ISBN (paperback): 978-1-7343885-0-3
ISBN (ebook): 978-1-7343885-2-7
Library of Congress Control Number: 2020901329

First edition

In memory of my grandma, Nancy Lodema Mashburn Herbert,
and my grandpa, Lafayette Alexander Herbert.

To my kids, grandkids, great-grandkids, and other "greats" in the
future: I wanted to provide a history of my youth so that you can
better understand who I am, what made me who I am, and what
molded my thoughts, morality, and philosophy of life.

And for Hana, wherever you are.

TABLE OF CONTENTS

INTRODUCTION

A Trip Back to Solve a Mystery

To celebrate our thirty-fifth anniversary in the spring of 2014, my wife, Gloria, and I took a trip from the rain forest of western Washington to the desert of Arizona. I wanted to show her where I'd spent many of my formative moments, from birth to four and a half years, plus many returns throughout my childhood, until my last visit at the age of fifteen. I was also looking for the answer to what, for many people, is a simple question: Where was I born?

For my whole life, my mom had claimed that I was born in Globe, Arizona. But I'd discovered that we hadn't moved to Globe proper until I was eighteen months old, so that didn't add up. Even my grandfather—her father—had a different story.

Over the years, I'd asked her about this discrepancy a hundred times, and she always either ignored me or changed the subject. Instead of diverting me, however, this only made me more suspicious. It wasn't until she was ninety-nine years old that I finally got her to talk about my birth.

It was a typical sunny Southern California day during the Thanksgiving weekend of 2012, and I was helping Mom go through some old family photos and papers when I came across the maternity ward bill for the birth of my youngest sister, Phyllis, who is ten years my junior. The bill was for a one-week stay, at $7.50 per day.

"The maternity ward where I was born must have been real cheap," I said, examining the worn sheet of paper.

"No, you were born at home," Mom said, then quickly changed the subject per usual. And, per usual, I repeated the question. I had little expectation of getting a different answer this time, but, as those close to me might say, I never do know when to quit!

"Why was I born at home?" I asked for the hundred and first time.

"Oh, that's just the way it was done in those days," she said. Even this little tidbit counted as new information. Treading carefully, I tried my luck with a follow-up question.

"Where were you and Dad living when I was born?"

"Globe," she said. I was disappointed by Mom's response, but I'd come this far, and damned if I'd just let it drop.

"I remember you saying that Dad got a job in the copper mines and so we moved to Globe proper when I was eighteen months old. So where *exactly* was I born?"

"It was just outside of Globe."

"Which direction?" Like a persistent prosecutor, I continued to lead the witness. "It was east of Globe, wasn't it?"

I knew I had her. Mom had, for over half a century, dodged my question about my birthplace, but finally the truth was going to come out.

"Yes, in a railroad maintenance camp just east of Globe."

"Oh really," I said, turning the screws. I knew that Dad had been a foreman of a crew of gandy dancers (railroad maintenance workers) that was responsible for the repair and upkeep of the Eastern Arizona Railroad tracks that just so happened to run through the 560 square miles of the San Carlos Apache Indian Reservation between Globe and Safford. "So you're saying I was born among the railroad crew, in a group of camp cars right there on a sidetrack?"

Mom cleared this up in a hurry. Class and social status were important to her, and she didn't want me to under-value their living situation. "Your dad and I lived in a nice little house. *Those* kinds of living cars were for the crew that worked for your dad."

"OK, so why does my birth certificate give Globe as my place of birth?"

"Our mailing address was in Globe, and the doctor that delivered you was from Globe. And that's enough questions for today!"

Why, you may be wondering, was my mom so enigmatic when it came to the subject of my birthplace? I think it has to do with the fact that my mom was prejudiced, something she'd be the first to admit. She was a wonderful person in many ways, but because of this less-than-admirable trait, she didn't want to acknowledge that I had been born on the San Carlos Indian Reservation, the western boundary of which is a few miles east of Globe.

And so it wasn't until right before her death that my mother finally gave up some long-guarded information about my birth. Even so, there remained unknowns. I'd hoped that this trip with Gloria would answer my birthplace question once and for all.

We spent the last few days traveling through Gila Valley in eastern Arizona, a stretch of green along the Gila River.

We visited Bryce, a blip of a town that is unique for not having any commerce. Its only claim to fame is that it was named after my great-great-grandfather Ebenezer Bryce. You might have heard of him—there's a national park called Bryce Canyon National Park in southern Utah, which is also his namesake.

Bryce had grown some since I had last been there, with a few farmhouses and a lot of cotton farms. The two tourist attractions are Ebenezer's original house, which is occupied, so you can't visit it, and Bryce Cemetery, which is also occupied, but you can visit. (The dead, unlike the living, aren't in a position to complain.) The cemetery is up a rough dirt road with deep ruts cut by rainwater looking for a path to the Gila River. It is best traversed with a Land Rover or some other vehicle with heavy-duty four-wheel drive. We were driving our 2012 Acura sedan, which, if it could think (it is a computer on wheels, after all, so I sometimes think it can), I'm sure it would have thought we were out of our freaking minds as we steered it onto the road. Somehow, it carried us up without too much struggle.

We made it to the top of the small desert hill with the wrought-iron arch and "Bryce Cemetery" spelled out on top. After letting the dust settle, Gloria and I got out. The sun was high in the endless expanse of blue sky, so different from the low, gray skies I'd grown accustomed to in the Pacific Northwest.

On the other side of the arch was a cemetery straight out of an old Western movie. Rounded mounds of dirt and small rocks shaped each grave, which were surrounded by typical dry desert grass, sagebrush, an ocotillo cactus or two, and a few mesquite trees. The most prominent graves in the cemetery were those of Ebenezer and Mary Bryce. Their graves were marked with an eight-foot monument and enclosed in a decorative six-foot-high wrought-iron fence. Blowing sands and heavy flash-flood downpours over the past hundred-plus years had eroded the engraving on the monument, making it difficult to read, though some kind soul had added a more-modern headstone to let everyone know that Bryce Canyon was named after this particular cemetery resident. Surprisingly, the cemetery is still in operation, with recently etched modern headstones and fresh flowers decorating some of the graves.

From Bryce we crossed the Gila River back to Pima, turned right onto Highway 70, and headed west toward Globe. Driving the next fifteen miles between Pima and Fort Thomas should have been like going down memory lane for me. Here was where my oldest memories first developed, then were embellished and reinforced by visits off and on until my fifteenth year. But, to my disappointment, the memory cues were missing. The little town of Glenbar was gone, as was Ashurst, the farming community in which my grandparents—the Bryces and the Herberts—had lived. Both had been replaced by large white fields of cotton waiting to be picked. There were no small country stores, houses, or buildings of any kind; the railroad tracks were still there, but gone were the water tower for the steam engines and the platforms for passengers boarding or disembarking and for unloading equipment ordered through the Sears catalog. Gone were Uncle Dewey's store and the elementary school, which also served as the only church in the area. It was as if someone took a big Mr. Clean Magic Eraser and wiped history clean.

There was one visible landmark still remaining: Ashurst Cemetery, hidden up a winding dirt road on top of a hill. Our car again heroically made the drive, and we found a cemetery similar to the Bryce Cemetery, maybe with a little more brown desert grass. Most of its residents were three generations of Bryces from my dad's side and Herberts from my mom's side. It continues to be an active cemetery; an aunt and an uncle of mine were delivered in their coffins by pickup truck and buried there the year before our visit.

After spending some time walking among the markers and trying to make connections to those laid to rest, we headed toward Globe. There, we drove around the city looking for the old main street. As we passed by the Gila County Historical Society, a thought hit me: maybe someone there could fill us in about the location of the railroad maintenance camp in which my mom claimed I was born.

We parked, and once inside I approached the woman at the front desk and told her my name. A voice from another room called out, "Send them back here. I'm the one they want to talk to."

Gloria and I walked to the back, where we met Lynn Perry, as well as her husband, Vernon.

"Was your father Howard Bryce?" Lynn asked.

"Yes," I said.

"Well, that makes us second cousins." She didn't look old enough to be my dad's cousin; in fact, she looked to be at least ten to fifteen years younger than me. But then I did the math. My great-grandparents, Ebenezer Park and Helen Bryce, had had eleven children, and the oldest child was my grandfather, the youngest Lynn's mother.

"We're interested in getting information about a railroad maintenance facility east of Globe," I told my newfound cousin. "I believe that's where my parents lived when I was born."

"I recall that there used to be one out there," Vernon said, "but it's now at the bottom of San Carlos Lake."

Now, I know what you might be thinking, and no, my mom wasn't behind the flooding of the maintenance camp. Even Mom wouldn't go to such great lengths to keep me from finding out where I was born. Also submerged was the village of Geronimo, the Apache community named for the famous Native American who'd led a bloody revenge on Mexican villages after a surprise militia attack on his camp that left his mother, his wife, and his three children dead.

What actually happened was that in 1924, the Bureau of Indian Affairs (BIA) started construction of the 250-foot-high Coolidge Dam on the Gila River, to form a reservoir for irrigating over 100,000 acres of Native American land. It was dedicated by President Coolidge in March 1930, and from then on, the reservoir gradually filled. It took nearly fifty years to form a lake that was twenty-three miles long and two miles wide, a lake that now lies above the Eastern Arizona Railroad camp and the village of Geronimo. The BIA had proposed disinterring the bodies from the village's tribal burial grounds and moving them elsewhere, but the Apaches vehemently objected to what they considered desecration of the dead. To this day, those bodies lie deep under the reservoir, underneath a concrete slab.

Lynn typed away at her computer as we talked, pulling up all kinds of information about me and my folks. Stumbling onto her and Vernon was like hitting a gold mine. (Well, this was Globe, so I probably should say "copper mine.") She got into the Arizona state files and brought up my birth certificate. By comparing my birthdate with census data and family genealogy records, she was able to determine that I was most likely born on the San Carlos Indian Reservation. Other computer research placed the Eastern Arizona Railroad maintenance facility adjacent to the train stop for Geronimo.

Leaving the museum, I was convinced that I was born on the San Carlos Indian Reservation. After many decades of giving my legal birthplace as Globe, which is on my birth certificate, I now know where I was really born. A lifelong mystery solved.

CHAPTER 1

Origin Story: 1880s–1935

I have always been immensely proud of my true place of birth. What young boy wouldn't be proud to say that he was born on the same Indian reservation as Haskay-bay-nay-ntayl—better known as the Apache Kid,[1] a larger-than-life champion, the "renegade of renegades," a cultural icon, and an indigenous symbol of a shifting historical reality—and where the famous Apache leaders Geronimo (Goyaałé) and Cochise (K'uu-ch'ish) once lived? As a kid, I felt like I had a distant connection to these heroes of resistance, these leaders in the fight against the assault on the Apache culture, even though my presence, as a blond, blue-eyed boy with Scottish roots, attests to the state of affairs at the time of my arrival.

---

1. McKanna, Clare V. "Apache Kid (1860–01 January 1930?), Indian scout." *American National Biography. (September 2010)*: https://www.anb.org/view/10.1093/anb/9780198606697.001.0001/anb-9780198606697-e-2091925.

That's right; I was born on the San Carlos Apache Indian Reservation. While my mom denied this, my dad's family openly and even proudly talked about our having an Apache ancestor on my grandfather Bryce's side. Their stories vary somewhat, but none doubted this particular lineage. My grandfather told me outright that I had been born on the San Carlos Indian Reservation; later my uncle took me with him to visit an Apache family on the reservation whom he introduced as relatives.

When I got older, I knew Apache kids, but not *the* Apache Kid, who'd been on the lam since 1889 and was widely accepted as dead. There were reports as late as 1935, however, that the legendary Apache Kid had snuck in to visit friends at San Carlos. That would have been two years after my birth.

Being born in the same place that such feared renegades once lived gave me status as a primary-grade kid, though I am sorry to say I can't claim to be one of those friends the Apache Kid might have visited, nor could my parents. I wonder what my warrior rating would have been if he had just stopped by to say *"dagot'ee shiteké atéé"* (roughly, "hello, my friend").

GO WEST, NEW CONVERTS, GO WEST

I was part of the first generation of my family born in the area. My parents had met as kids in Ashurst, a small rural community in the Gila Valley, about ten miles southeast of the reservation border. My mom, Louise (Herbert) Bryce, was born in 1913 in Commerce, Georgia, one of eleven children (nine of whom survived childhood). My dad, Carlos

Bryce, who went by his middle name of Howard, was born in Bryce, Arizona Territory, in 1910, the eldest child of eleven.

Ashurst had been settled by Mormons who had been sent by the church in the late 1870s from Utah. Dad's great-grandparents and ten of their eleven children and their families, along with a hundred head of livestock, arrived in the valley in 1881. Meanwhile, my mom's family was living in South Carolina. Her parents, two uncles, an aunt, and their spouses, and their families were converted to the Mormon Church in the early 1900s. It was rough being the only Mormons living among devout Southern Baptists, so Grandpa and Grandma Herbert decided to move to Georgia, hoping that life would be better there. Instead, they felt the same pressure they had in South Carolina; it was especially hard on their children. So in 1924, Mom's parents and their six kids, ages three to fifteen, and their married seventeen-year-old daughter, her husband, and their nine-month-old son joined two of Grandpa's brothers, a brother-in-law, and their wives and kids. This big group packed their belongings into a Buick, an Overland, and three Model T Fords and left the beautiful green states of Georgia and South Carolina to come to the arid high desert of Gila Valley in southeastern Arizona.

The trip's entire 1,800 miles of road were unpaved and either dusty or muddy, depending on the weather. Motels hadn't been invented yet, so they camped out every night underneath the stars. (The word *motel*, a contraction of "motor hotel," originates from the Milestone Mo-Tel of San Luis Obispo, California, which was built in 1925.) If the group was able to find a spot near a river or creek to make camp, they would stay an extra day to do laundry, wash dishes, take much-needed baths, and try catching a few fish for dinner and breakfast.

Mom's family stopping for the night on the way to Ashurst, Arizona, in 1924.

After this long and arduous journey, the Herbert family reached the Gila Valley and chose to settle 160 acres of land that were available for homesteading in Ashurst. In part, it was simply logistics—the Native Americans had been run out, and the land was open to white settlers. More important, it was where my great-uncle Dewey Bryce, the missionary who was responsible for converting the Herberts, lived.

And so the Herbert family and the Bryce family came to occupy two homesteads facing each other across a dusty, unpaved road in southeastern Arizona.

ABSENCE MAKES THE HEART GROW FONDER . . . FOR SOMEONE ELSE

In 1924, the year my parents met, my mom was eleven and my dad was fourteen. Soon they would be more than just neighbors. Dad had been dating Mom's older sister Stella, but as soon as she left to go on a Mormon mission, Mom swooped in. They eloped to Lordsburg, New Mexico, in the fall of 1931, just a few months after my mom left high school. (She'd always told me that she and my dad had graduated from high school, but I discovered during the writing of this book that this probably wasn't true. While going through a box of old pictures and papers Mom gave me a couple of months before she died, I found a sheet of paper in her handwriting stating that she and Dad had finished high school at the end of their junior year. While doing more research, I learned that in those days, the senior year was for students going on to college.)

Mom was an extrovert but also profoundly insecure; she enjoyed life and being at the center of attention, yet she was always worried that people were speaking poorly of her. To this day I still remember some of the wackiest sayings that would pop out of her mouth, like "Hotter than a two-dollar pistol," "Slicker than a slimy snail," "Handy as a pocket in a shirt," "He has more money than Carter has little liver pills," "He's as crazy as a June bug," and "Enough room for a dead man and a monkey." She would also sing crazy songs from the turn of the twentieth century and tell funny stories about herself—funnier, in my opinion, than those of the comedian Phyllis Diller. She loved to dance, and she also made a wicked lemon-cream meringue pie.

Dad was a mellow, even-keeled guy with a subtle sense of humor and a kind heart. He took life as it came. In fact, I remember him yelling only to get immediate attention for matters of safety; otherwise, he used discussions, not arguments or reprimands, to get his point across.

Mom always said that Dad was a "jack-of-all-trades and a master of romance." He never forgot flowers on special

occasions, but he believed that *real* romance is about showing love at unexpected times. If he was walking and came
upon a single daisy or Johnny-jump-up along the road, he'd
pick it and bring it home to Mom—to his way of thinking,
that was far better than a dozen roses on Valentine's Day.

I don't know much about my parents' first years of marriage, before I came along. They were young and in love,
excited about making a home together, and hopeful about
my dad's prospects for work, even as the global economy
tanked. I entered this world in November 1933, just as it
reached its lowest point financially in hundreds of years.
The stock market had crashed in October 1929, which sent
Wall Street into a panic and wiped out millions of investors.
Over nine thousand banks failed during the 1930s, with four
thousand giving up the ghost in 1933 alone. With the Great
Depression in full swing, unemployment was at an all-time
high at 25 percent, meaning one out of four workers could
not find a job.

Not that I was aware of any of this at the time. I was
just a baby, after all, and I had more important things, like
learning to walk and talk and get into trouble, on my mind.

MY FIRST MOVES

We moved to Globe proper shortly before I turned two. Dad
had managed to avoid the unemployment line and had been
working as a railroad crew foreman on location fifty miles to
the southeast, but he'd lined up a new job in one of the copper mines in Globe. I don't know if he'd been laid off, or if,
by that time, the reservoir had started to overtake the maintenance camp, or if it was because Eastern Arizona Railroad
had merged with the Southern Pacific Railroad, or if Mom

just wanted off the reservation (which she claimed she had never lived on in the first place). It could have been simply that the copper-mine job paid better. Whatever the reason, it was time to pick up and go, something we would do many, many times during my childhood.

Globe was the biggest city in Gila County, with a population of just over seven thousand. Legend has it that it was named for a globe-shaped piece of pure silver discovered in the area.[2] I don't have much to tell about living there— after all, what can you expect of the recall of a two-year-old? Those memory cells hadn't developed yet. Mom, however, had a couple of stories she liked to tell, so I do have the memories of her telling them, and sometimes I can imagine my toddler self in the tale.

As one story goes: One day, my cousin Nancy, who was a few months younger than me, tried to pick me up and proceeded to drop me headfirst. I landed with a smack, square on my face, breaking my brand-new front tooth. I had to live with the gap where that tooth should have been, plus the teasing that came with it, for the next five or six years, until I turned seven and my permanent tooth finally grew in.

Another story was about me playing in the coal bin. Houses back then were often heated with a coal-burning furnace, and apparently I liked to play in the coal that was stored in an open bin outside, on the north side of the house. My guess is that I wanted to look like my dad did when he came home from the copper mine. Cell phones were more than half a century in the future, but I'm sure we would have made a good like-father-like-son selfie.

While playing in coal might be fun for a two-year-old, mining for copper is dirty and difficult. So, a year or so later,

---

2. "Globe Information," City of Globe (website), http://www.globeaz.gov/visitors/information.

Dad was ready for something new. The construction of the Bartlett Dam on the Verde River was underway, and there was a call for construction workers. The pay was good—better than in the mines—and working in the fresh air beat working in a long, deep, dark tunnel, blasting and extracting copper ore from the belly of a mountain.

So we moved again, traveling over a hundred miles to the northeast. To Mom, there was one big downside to this move: Carl Lee, one of Dad's buddies from high school, had also gotten a job working on the dam, and together they enjoyed a cheap cigar and a beer or two after work on payday. As a fourth-generation Mormon, Dad was a little looser with the rules and didn't see the harm of having a drink and a puff on a Friday afternoon after work. But Mom, a first-generation Mormon convert, liked to stick to the religious strictures, and she was none too happy about their extracurricular activities. This led to some ill-tempered discussions, mainly with my mom loudly proclaiming her need to protect her innocent little boy from the evils of alcohol and tobacco. This ongoing conflict might have been a reason why, the next time we visited my maternal grandparents' farm, my parents left me there.

CHAPTER 2

Down on the Farm: 1936–1937

I loved living with Grandpa and Grandma Herbert on the farm. My maternal grandmother, Nancy Lodema (Mashburn) Herbert, was born on February 22, 1889, in Homer, Georgia. There are no records of her education level, but I was told that she'd made it through the fifth grade. My maternal grandfather, Lafayette Alexander (he later called himself F. A., after shortening his first name to Fate) Herbert, was born on May 2, 1887, in Fort Madison, South Carolina, and made it through the second grade. The two of them got married in 1905, then together converted to Mormonism ten years later.

My grandparents were good hard-working people, the epitome of "salt of the earth." Grandma was one of the kindest, warmest, most loving people I was ever lucky enough to know. I can't recall a single time that she said a bad word about anyone, and she didn't buy into the era's child-rearing philosophy of "spare the rod and spoil the child." If you did anything worthy of punishment, she would say in a soft but stern voice, "Do you know what you did that was wrong?" Usually the answer was yes. "What was it that you did that you shouldn't have done?" she'd then ask. That's when you had the chance to plead your case. If you were contrite enough and said you were sorry in a convincing way, you might get a dismissal. If not, she would tell you to "go find a switch of appropriate size." Once you returned, she'd ask, "How many swats do you think is right for what you did?" The swats themselves were always very mild. Hers was a psychological punishment: picking out the switch and deciding on the number of swats you deserved was more than enough to get the lesson across.

At six feet two inches and 240 pounds of pure muscle, Grandpa provided a stark contrast to Grandma's more-diminutive demeanor. He worked hard, and he expected those working alongside him to do the same. To Grandpa, a promise was a commitment that you kept, and his firm handshake was as good as his signature. He was truly a self-made farmer, and he enjoyed the work; he believed that the land and the animals "talked" to him.

When I arrived in 1936, Grandpa still had a couple of Percheron draft horses, giant beasts approximately six feet tall at the front shoulders and weighing about 2,000 pounds. Unlike some of his tractor-driving neighbors, he used them to plow the one-acre vegetable garden; he claimed that the horse-drawn plow did less damage than a tractor and that they could better get into the corners.

I remember having to practically run to keep up with him as he strode around the farm. Though I was only three when I arrived and four when I left, that was when I stopped being a baby and started becoming a boy. I'm pretty sure

Grandpa didn't realize just how young I was—he fully expected even a little tyke like me to help out.

THE HERBERTS' HUMBLE HOME

The town of Ashurst was a place where people trusted their neighbors and felt safe letting their kids roam free. A place and a time when a trusting grandmother would let her three-year-old grandson walk to the neighbors' farm or even down to Uncle Dewey's store, if he promised to only walk off to the side and never, ever, ever on the road. "Go out to the henhouse and take a couple of eggs down to Uncle Dewey's," she'd say. He, in exchange, would "pay" me with a handful of jelly beans out of the candy jar.

Dewey Bryce, postmaster, farmer, and owner of the only store in Ashurst, lived around the corner and approximately a quarter of a mile southeast on Highway 70. His family's home and farm were behind the small country mercantile, which also housed the post office in the front corner and had a gas pump out front. The name I remember on the front of the store was "United States Post Office—Ashurst, Arizona," but everyone just called it "Uncle Dewey's store." His wife, my aunt Hazel, was mainly responsible for running the store, and she also held the title of assistant postmaster and so she had the authority to take over Uncle Dewey's postal duties in his absence. He was gone a lot because he spent most of his time running the farm.

My grandparents' farm was adjacent to US Highway 70, with the house a couple hundred feet east and facing Ashurst Road. The house was very, very modest, a rectangular box with a gabled roof and walls made of "barn boards," otherwise known as reclaimed lumber. There's an

old saying: "Too proud for whitewash, too poor for paint."
Well, my grandparents weren't too proud for whitewash, or
calcimine, a low-cost type of paint made from slaked lime—
calcium hydroxide, $Ca(OH)_2$, and chalk (calcium carbonate,
$CaCO_3$)—that cures through a reaction with carbon dioxide
in the atmosphere to form calcium carbonate in the form
of calcite. (This fact is something I'd learn much later, once
I got interested in chemistry.) Its use is sometimes called
"whiting." By the time I got there, the heavy rains had
washed off most of the latest application of whitewash, so to
a preschooler, it looked a lot like plain old bare wood.

The house sat in the southeast corner of the farmyard,
alongside the kitchen garden and about twenty feet back
from Ashurst Road. Grandma had gone to great lengths to
dress up the front of the house with a flower garden that
blossomed in a riot of color with the spring rains and faded
just as quickly as the scorching summer weather set in.
When in bloom, the garden was an oasis of hollyhocks, dai-
sies, zinnias, and pansies amidst the bare brown dirt surrounding the house.

There was a small irrigation ditch parallel to the road,
and a footbridge with no handrails leading across to the mail-
box. Deeply rooted into the bank of the ditch was a majestic
old cottonwood tree. It managed to escape becoming fire-
wood by offering additional beautification to the front of the
house, plus a big limb perfect for hosting a swing, and, most
of all, by providing cooling shade. That was my grandma's
favorite place to relax.

When I close my eyes, in my mind I see a beautiful,
peaceful scene. There sits, on the edge of the footbridge over
the irrigation ditch, my forty-eight-year-old grandmother,
the mother of eleven children, underneath that big tree, just
enjoying the shade, her knitting basket beside her. She is

knitting a sweater, swinging her feet back and forth, and half humming, half singing a song to herself. My aunt Maxine sits in the swing, whirling around and around in circles. And there I am, a little boy with a lot of energy, running around trying to catch butterflies, too young to understand that you can't catch butterflies by chasing them.

FOR RUNNING WATER, TIP BUCKET

The house only had four rooms. It was a tight fit for seven people: Grandma and Grandpa, sixteen-year-old Talmage, fifteen-year-old Callis, ten-year-old Falene, six-year-old Maxine, and three-year-old me. The largest room, or what today we might call "the great room," was the hub of indoor activity. It contained the kitchen, with a cast-iron wood-burning stove for both cooking and heating the house, a large table, and lots of chairs, including a couple of wooden rockers. There was a parlor, where the grown-ups went to visit with other grown-ups, unless the visitors were church officials—then the kids would have to troop in and be sure to remember to behave ourselves. On Saturday nights, the boys took refuge in the parlor while the girls bathed (then vice versa) in an approximately thirty-inch-diameter number 3 galvanized metal tub brought in and placed between the cupboard and the kitchen stove in the great room. (It was the same tub that Grandma used on Mondays for laundry; more on that later.) The tub's proximity to the stove kept the water warm, and near to additional water being heated on the woodstove. It also gave some privacy. When it was Grandma's turn, the tub was emptied and replaced with fresh water, and when she was finished, Grandpa got in. If the weather was warm enough and there was water in the irrigation ditch, the boys, and sometimes me, would grab a bar of soap and bathe in the ditch.

The entrance to the two bedrooms—one for my grandparents and one for us kids—was just off the main room. In the spring, summer, and early fall, my teenage uncles Talmage and Callis avoided the crowd and slept outside under the stars on a metal-framed bed. Boy, was I ever jealous. Still, I knew that someday I'd be big enough to sleep outside, too.

No, I did not forget to mention the bathroom. That's because there was no bathroom. There was also no running water. A well was not feasible, since the aquifer was several hundred feet below and we had no electrical power for a pump. So, when in Ashurst, do as the Ashurstians do: dig a cistern. All of the water we used for domestic purposes came by bucket from that cistern, located about ten feet outside the kitchen door.

The cistern was approximately four feet in diameter and twelve feet deep, lined with large river rocks cemented in place. It had a concrete lid with a two-foot hole in the center, covered by a fifty-five-gallon drum with both ends removed and sealed to the concrete so that nothing at ground level could get in. The top of the drum was kept covered with a wooden lid. It could hold a little over a thousand gallons of water.

As you might imagine, refilling the cistern was a major event. Once the water was nearly gone, we'd fill up a couple of ten-gallon milk cans with the remaining water for domestic use for the next few days, then scrub and wipe down the cistern's interior walls with rags dipped in a mixture of bleach and water.

Grandma and I. I'm the one sitting on the cistern lid.

Only Grandpa was allowed to go down into the cistern, so he was the one to do all that cleaning and sanitizing.

Talmage and Callis worked above, one drawing buckets full of the last of the water up and lowering supplies down for Grandpa, while the other used the last bit of water on Grandma's flowers and what little grass there was in the front yard. Finally, it would be declared ready for the refill, and I was the lucky boy who got to go with Grandpa to get the water. He would start up the tractor, and I'd jump on the back, wrap my arms around his waist, and away we'd go.

We'd cross the road over to Grandpa Bryce's farm, hook up his tank wagon, and then head out across Highway 70 and the railroad tracks, turning right to follow the tracks to the railroad's water tower. Grandpa parked the tank wagon as close to the water tower as he could, then jumped up on the wagon, opened the lid on top, swung the water delivery spout around over the opening, and pulled the chain on the delivery valve. I watched in awe as a great gushing waterfall flowed into the tank. When the tank was full, he closed the valve, swung the spout back in place, closed the lid, jumped off the wagon, climbed on the tractor, started it up, and yelled at me, "Come, let's go!" Back on the farm, he and his sons would fill up the cistern. The cows, horses, and pigs would look on calmly; any leftover water would be emptied into the livestock's watering trough.

THE BEST LITTLE OUTHOUSE IN ASHURST

As far as our lack of indoor plumbing went, the thousand-gallon cistern compensated in terms of our water supply. But we still needed somewhere to put all that water . . . once it had been drunk.

The outhouse was about thirty feet behind the house, between the barn and the kitchen garden. It was known far and wide (or so I thought at the time) as the best outhouse in Ashurst, a "three holer" with the knotholes and spaces between the siding boards covered by slats and "tin" can lids, so no one could peek in. It also had a couple of screened vents up high to let air and light in and, more important, to let the smell escape and keep the flies out. It even had a shelf for the old Sears Roebuck, Montgomery Ward, and J. C. Penney's catalogs, which we relegated to toilet-paper status whenever the newer catalogs arrived in the mail. (These catalogs also served another purpose: educating me about women's underwear!) There was also an old bucket filled with ashes, which Grandpa refilled from the woodstove and laundry fire pit whenever it started to run low. (I didn't know what its purpose was until I was a teenager. The ash helps decrease odors, reduce insects, and absorb liquids.)

Grandpa had built a special hole for kids that was lower to the ground, in addition to the two adult holes, one a little bigger than the other. None had a seat or cover; these were just ovals with the edges rounded smooth with a wood file and sandpaper.

Grandma, trying to get me to establish a routine, would send me to the outhouse shortly after Grandpa headed out to work in the fields and my aunts and uncles left for school. Looking back, I really think it was just a ploy to get me out of the house so she could have some time to herself. Sitting there in the outhouse, waiting for things to happen, also gave my mind lots of time to wander—and for me to get up to mischief.

Perhaps you might be wondering, as I did: Why three holes? This is something that I pondered many times throughout my early childhood. Having two holes, one for kids and one for grown-ups—now that made sense. But why did the big people get two holes? That seemed like overkill.

Maybe there were two holes so that two people could use the outhouse at the same time? That seemed strange, and I couldn't ever remember seeing two people go in or come out of the outhouse together. On the other hand, I'd seen Grandpa holding Grandma's hand and carrying a lantern to light the way as they walked to the outhouse together one night. Did they go in together or didn't they?

Then there was the puzzle of who used which hole. Did my aunt Maxine, who was seven but short, use the kids' hole or one of the bigger ones, and if so, which one? Was the smaller grown-ups' hole for Grandma and the other women, and the bigger one for Grandpa and the other men? I spent many a stretch ruminating on such grand philosophical questions.

Eventually I decided that the big one was for Grandpa, and that the small potty hole was specially designed for yours truly, while everyone else had to use the middle one. This theory would soon get me into trouble.

One day, thinking I was a big boy, I decided to use what I assumed to be Grandpa's hole instead of the low-level one. I was all alone, where no one could see what I was doing, and so I climbed up onto the biggest hole. Boy, was that ever a mistake!

I sat my bare bottom on the edge of the hole, then scooted back to position it over the hole—and I damn near fell in! For the one terrifying moment when my butt dropped down, I thought I was going to fall straight into the swampy pit full of my relatives' poop, pee, used torn-out catalog pages, and wood ash that was just waiting four feet below for me to make a big, stinking splash. Instead, thank goodness, I was just barely too big.

Now that I knew that I wasn't going to fall in, I could focus on the real problem: being caught inside the hole. There

I was, scared nearly to death, with my back pressed against the back side of the hole and my legs almost straight up in the air, making a "V" shape with my body. Crazy thoughts ran through my head: What if, while trying to free myself, I ended up falling in for real this time? How deep would I sink in all that crap? How was my family going to find me with the door locked? If someone did get in, would they poop or pee on me, or would they hear me floating around down there? How were they going to get me out? Was it possible to drown in poop? Wouldn't my mom be so mad if I did?

I refused to find out the answers to what were, given the situation, very reasonable questions. With a lot of wiggling and thrashing, I was finally able to get ahold of the edge of the other big people's hole and pull myself out.

Some people say, "Never bite off more than you can chew." I would add, "Never sit on a hole too big for your bottom."

ANOTHER OUTHOUSE SURPRISE

That wasn't my only outhouse melodrama. Another time, while waiting for nature to take its course, I was having an involved discussion with one of my imaginary friends. Of course, I was voicing both sides of the conversation, making my voice low and then answering back in my more natural tone.

My imaginary friend and I were having a good long dialogue when, out of the blue, my mother's voice called out loud and clear.

"Who's in there with you? Who are you talking to?"

She scared me so bad, I damn near fell in the hole again!

After collecting myself, I yelled back, "I'm in here all by myself!"

"I know someone else is there," she said. "I can hear their voice!" The door started to rattle, and Mom's voice got louder. "Unlock the door this instant!" But instead of waiting for me to follow her order, she jogged the door so hard that she jarred the lock loose! The door swung out with a bang.

All she found was one little boy with his shorts and pants down around his ankles and a big smirk on his face.

"See," I said, "I told you that no one was in here but me."

What a way to find out that your mother had come to visit.

MY FIRST FUNERAL

I was overjoyed to see Mom and Dad, but the occasion wasn't a happy one. I quickly learned that Dad's dad, Carl Bryce, had just died, a couple of weeks shy of my fourth birthday. His death was the first I had ever experienced. I remember Dad and two of his brothers, Ebbie and Bill, digging Grandpa Bryce's grave, lowering the coffin in, and filling the grave with dirt. It was a pick-and-shovel job, out there in the boot-hill-style cemetery, with wooden grave markers at the heads of mounds of rocks and dirt. Ebbie had made the coffin; it had three two-by-fours across the bottom, and they used ropes for lowering the coffin so that they could be removed easily. I remember standing there not with sadness or grief about my grandfather's death—I wasn't as close to him as I was to my mom's parents, and I was too young to really understand what was happening—but in awe of the mechanics.

I was always interested in the "why" of things, and my dad and maternal grandfather were very patient and good at explaining. They also knew when to suggest that I figure it out for myself. I don't remember if I asked about how Ebbie made the coffin or how they rigged up the system for lowering it, but I do remember this early lesson in engineering.

A WITCH ON LAUNDRY DAY

On the farm, Monday was laundry day. Grandma had a neat setup for getting seven people's dusty dresses and muddy overalls and sweaty socks clean. Grandpa had built a porch-like platform with a roof, which held the washer and a table big enough to hold two washtubs for rinsing. Grandma used soap she'd made from animal fat and store-bought lye, and she would heat the water in a smoke-blackened galvanized washtub over an outdoor fire pit before adding it to the Maytag washer, which had a gas engine. Beyond running the washing machine, that engine served a second purpose.

Generally, we used coal oil lamps for everyday lighting. Since the mid-1800s, lamp oil had evolved from whale oil, rendered from whale blubber; to coal oil, refined from cannel coal (a type of soft coal); to kerosene, refined from petroleum (crude oil). Price was the main factor in this evolution—it takes a lot of resources to hunt whales! Then Abraham Gesner came along, in 1854, and registered Kerosene as a trademark, granting only two companies the right to call their lamp oil Kerosene with a capital "K." Thus the same type of lamp oil was sold as both the brand-name Kerosene and "coal oil." To add to the confusion, in 1851, Samuel Kier began selling lamp oil he refined from petroleum as "carbon oil." (Seems like instead of reinventing the wheel, people just rename it!) Eventually, Gesner lost his trademark when his company was absorbed into the petroleum monopoly Standard Oil, and with that kerosene lost its capital "K," becoming a generic name for lamp oil, stove oil, and, later on, jet fuel.

All that to say that most days we used coal oil lamps, which had a distinct smell and produced a lot of smoke. That's all well and good when it's just family, but on special occasions when guests were coming over, Grandpa would hook up the washing machine engine's drive belt to a small generator to give us electricity for half a dozen or so light bulbs in the parlor and great room.

One Monday, Grandma was gathering the wash for laundry day when she remembered that she had loaned out her washboard.

"Herbie," she called, "go on down to your aunt Ida's farm and ask for my washboard." My grandma knew that assigning these kinds of tasks makes a little kid feel important.

The farm was about four hundred yards down the road. *No problem,* I thought, happy to take on such a big-boy job. I walked proudly, my head held high. But just as I neared the farmhouse, a woman stuck her head out the upstairs window. She was in a cotton nightgown, with uncombed fuzzy gray hair, no teeth, and not a trace of color in her face. With a raspy voice, she screeched, "Hi, Herbie!"

Terrified, I turned on my heel and ran all the way back home.

Grandma was outside on the washing platform, just minding her own business, when I nearly barreled into her. "There's a witch!" I yelled at the top of my lungs. "There's a witch at Aunt Ida's house!"

Grandma had decades of experience dealing with her gaggle of kids and grandkids, and this announcement didn't faze her one bit. In fact, and to my consternation, she just chuckled.

"That was Aunt Ida," she said after a moment. "Remember how she wasn't at church last Sunday? That's because she was sick. She's probably not well just yet. Come on, I'll go with you. We can see how she's feeling, and you can carry the washboard back."

"I don't want to go," I whined. "I'm afraid of the witch."

"There's no witch, Herbie," Grandma repeated. "That was *Aunt Ida*. She probably just hasn't prettied herself up this morning. She'll be pretty when we get there, you'll see."

Reluctantly, I followed Grandma back down the road. I didn't want to be a scaredy-cat, after all, and I mostly trusted that my grandmother wouldn't deliver me straight into the hands of a witch. But still—the lady had no teeth!

Indeed, Grandma was right. By the time we got there, Aunt Ida had brushed her hair, put in her false teeth, dabbed on a little makeup, and had covered up her pajamas with a chenille bathrobe.

Even so, once we got back home with the washboard, I still had some doubts—Aunt Ida and the crazy lady with her head out the window didn't look like the same person to me.

CAN I HAVE MY TEETH BACK?

In a rural part of a country still reeling from the Great Depression, for many people it wasn't always possible to go to a dentist. And, more than that, not every dentist was what we'd consider legitimate by today's standards. So Aunt Ida was far from being the only one who relied on a set of false teeth.

One day, I was out playing near the barn and spotted an empty fifty-five-gallon barrel. I looked around—Grandpa was out in the field with some farmhands, and Grandma was in the garden. My aunts and uncles had left for school a while earlier. I listened for a moment; the only sound I heard was cows mooing contentedly in the distance.

Too short to climb into the thirty-five-inch-high barrel, I found a wooden box and dragged it over, then used it to climb up and in, dropping down to land on my feet with a thud. Suddenly, my world was limited to the interior of the barrel, with a bright-white sun shining overhead. Clearly, I hadn't thought this situation all the way through; had I done so, I would have realized that if I needed a box to get in, I was going to need one to get out. So there I was, stuck not in an outhouse potty hole this time but inside a barrel. Not as stinky, but still not ideal.

The new farmhand must have been heading from the outhouse back out to the field and heard strange noises coming from the barrel, because a deep voice suddenly said, "What are you doing down there?" When I looked up, I saw a stranger with his false teeth pushed partway out of his mouth with his tongue. This was not the savior I'd been hoping for.

I started screaming.

Grandma and I were very close, and she was very protective of me. She must have heard me all the way from the garden, and she came running. Let me tell you, you don't want to mess with Nancy Herbert's favorite grandson. She might have been only five feet six inches, but the new farmhand met his match that day.

Unfortunately, when Grandma started yelling and pounding on his back, his teeth fell clear out of his mouth and into the barrel. My barrel. The barrel that I was trapped in, now with the addition of a set of false teeth. That was when I went berserk.

"Get out of here!" Grandma yelled at the farmhand, pushing him away. "You're scaring my grandson!"

"I need to get my teeth," the farmhand said.

"Herbie, Herbie, calm yourself!" she said to me. "I can't get you out of there unless you calm down."

I kept screaming.

"I need to get my teeth," the farmhand said.

I was still screaming.

"Get out of here!" Grandma yelled.

"But my teeth!" the farmhand said. "I need my teeth!"

Finally, my grandma said, "Go tell Mr. Herbert that I fired you, and while you're at it, tell him why. You'll need to settle on how much he owes you for this morning. You can come back by here on your way off the farm—your teeth will be sitting right here on this box."

CHAPTER 3

A Forest of My Own: 1938

I don't remember saying goodbye, or whether it even felt like a goodbye at the time. My grandparents were like my parents, and my actual parents were also like my parents, so when Mom and Dad came to get me, I'm not sure I felt like a separation was taking place. More like going from one loving home to another.

Dad had been offered a job in Coconino National Forest, southeast of Flagstaff, Arizona, by a logging company. It was either late winter or early spring when we arrived, with snow up to my pudgy knees and a bite in the air. Dad would be working temporarily as an auto mechanic until the logging camp opened, and so we lived in an auto court consisting of a circle of one-room cottages built out of large river rocks.

I remember walking through the snow with Mom to bring Dad his lunch. The going was tough; I could barely get my legs high enough to take a step, so after a few struggles, Mom tromped down a path through the snow so that

I could make it to the plowed street in front of our cottage. At the auto shop, we found Dad; or, rather, we found his legs sticking out from underneath a car down in the auto repair pit, a trouble light hanging overhead.

"Howard," Mom said, "Herbie and I are here with your lunch."

"Go ahead and put it on the workbench," my dad's disembodied voice called out. "I can't get out of here just yet."

"Mom," I whispered, pulling on her skirt, "the car's on top of Dad. It's going to squish him!"

Dad must have overheard, because he called out, "Come on over to the front of the car, Herbie. You see that small space there? You can squeeze through the opening, check to make sure I'm not being squished."

The owner of the shop, a large man with a smear of oil across his overalls, approached. "Look here, son, there's a ladder," he said. He held it as I descended into the darkness to find, to my relief, that my dad was indeed not squished. Once that matter was settled, I looked up. There, right above me, was the street-worn underbelly of an automobile, with its pipes and bolts and tanks and metal doodads. I'm sure my dad saw my eyes go big and my jaw drop, because he took a moment's pause to give me a quick lesson on what makes the wheels go around. All too soon, it was time for me to climb out of the pit so he could get back to work. To use my grandkids' vernacular: it was awesome.

OUR HOME IN THE FOREST

That spring, when the ground was starting to emerge from the snow and the dirt roads had become drivable, we moved to the ponderosa pine forest south of Mormon Lake, about halfway between Flagstaff and Oak Creek Canyon. Dad was to be the caretaker and maintenance man for the equipment at a log-loading yard. He would be responsible for keeping the trucks, Caterpillar equipment, and the generator running, and the loading crane lubed and operating.

At the end of the day, the loggers and truck drivers went home, leaving just Mom, Dad, and me way out there in the middle of the forest. Our small one-room house trailer was parked across from the maintenance yard and loading area, separated by a one-lane dirt road that extended past our house for a hundred yards or so. (All of the roads in that part of the forest were dirt.) I slept on the couch, while Mom and Dad turned the eating booth into a bed every night after dinner, folding it up again before breakfast. The tiny one-person kitchen had a two-burner coal oil stove next to the dishpan. There was no oven; Mom baked using a cast-iron Dutch oven on the stovetop.

We didn't have a refrigerator, and so our meals had to consist of foods that did not require refrigeration. At the same time, a quick trip to the store just to pick up fresh food was out of the question, since the closest store was over an hour's drive away. My mom, knowing that milk was important for kids to grow good teeth and strong bones, made sure we had plenty of canned evaporated milk on hand, to be reconstituted by mixing with water. My parents bought cans by the case, storing them underneath the trailer since there was no room inside. It became my job to go out and get a can or two when needed because I fit under the trailer better than Mom or Dad, or so they claimed. I don't have fond memories of that reconstituted milk we drank or poured on our breakfast cereal and corn bread. It was nothing compared to the cows' milk I'd had on Grandma and Grandpa's farm, which was so fresh that sometimes it was still warm, not having time to cool during its transit from the udder to my glass.

The subsistence farm in Ashurst that my dad had grown up on was much like my mom's—no surprise, since the two farms were right across the street from each other. Like most farms in the area, the Bryce farm had Jersey milk cows, a kitchen garden, chickens, and a pig or two. (Jersey milk is known as "buttery milk" because of its high butterfat content at 5.2 percent, compared to a Holstein's 3.5 percent. Most commercial milk comes from Holsteins, because of their high production, while Jersey milk is used mainly for butter and cheese. Yes, you can taste the difference.) Dad had developed a taste for farm-style comfort food, and to him, the pinnacle of good eating was corn bread cooked with the pork cracklings—the leftovers from fat being rendered to make lard—in a cast-iron frying pan, which adds a succulent fatty flavor and gives it a thick crust. I think that if Dad had been asked to define heaven, it would be: a big bowl of corn bread with cracklings baked in a cast-iron pan, covered with fresh raw milk from a Jersey cow; a plate on the side containing fresh tomatoes, green onions, radishes, cucumbers, bell peppers, and jalapeños, with cottage cheese sprinkled with fresh-ground pepper, and a small mound of salt to dip the veggies in; a glass of buttermilk; and for dessert, a large piece of lemon cream pie with meringue and another glass of milk. Is your mouth watering right now? Mine sure is. Ah, but I digress.

There was no running water at my new home in the forest, but I didn't mind—I'd gotten used to this state of affairs at my grandparents' farm. Instead of using a thousand-gallon cistern, we had to haul water from a nearby creek in ten-gallon milk cans. Our electricity came from the generator in the maintenance yard, which ran 24/7. I'm sure that the generator was meant to primarily provide floodlights for the maintenance and loading yard, with the side benefit of lighting the house trailer and the path to the outhouse.

I remember waking up one morning, right after we moved there, to find snow on the ground. Mom went outside in her nightgown and scooped up a panful of fresh snow, which she brought inside, and then added evaporated milk, sugar, and vanilla. Can't beat snow-made ice cream for breakfast. Afterward, Dad left for work, and Mom and I went out to play in the snow. We made a snowman using a pinecone for the nose, since no carrots were available. Then we lay down and made snow angels. Our angels looked like girl angels to me—a travesty!—so I made another one. This time I did not move my legs back and forth, and my new angel had two distinct legs instead of a skirt, so it was a boy angel.

A SQUIRREL TEACHES ME A LESSON

For a four-and-a-half-year-old boy, the woods were paradise. I considered the forest to the west side of our road and south of the logging road "mine." I had all the time in the world to explore, looking for trees to climb, for animal tracks in the dirt, for wild turkeys making their funny squawking sounds, for deer nibbling the shrubs. Another forest bonus: all the pine resin gum I could ever want. Dad had showed me how to find resin gum on pine trees and what it looked like when it was ready to be chewed. If I couldn't break it off with my fingers, then I used a small rock to chip it off. If it fell on the ground, Dad told me, I should wipe the dirt off on my pants before putting it in my mouth, because sand would harm my teeth. When I first started chewing the gum, it tasted like turpentine, but after a while, the awful taste was replaced by a flavor that matched the scent of pine, and I could chew to my heart's content.

I ran wild, and I let my imagination run wild, too. I spent a lot of effort chasing squirrels and chipmunks, trying my hardest to catch one for a pet. Most of the time they quickly outsmarted me, a lumbering giant whose tree-climbing skills must have seemed to them utterly graceless. I did manage to catch one, just one time, and I can tell you that I learned a valuable lesson.

One fine afternoon, I was playing in the woods when I spotted a squirrel a little ways down the path. I set off like a gunshot, chasing her up a small tree. She ran out on a limb, and, for some reason, there she froze. Perhaps she was paralyzed by fear, or maybe she had lured me into a trap. Either way, I caught her by the tail. That was when the lesson began: She twisted her body around and bit the side of my right hand, the hand I was holding her with. She sunk her little rodent teeth in, and I howled. *OK, OK, OK,* I thought, trying not to panic, *if I let go of her, she'll let go of me.*

Unfortunately, that squirrel didn't read my mind, or if she did, she didn't agree to my terms, and she certainly didn't play fair. I let go of her tail, but she held firm to my hand. I started shaking my hand, screaming and crying while also trying not to fall out of the tree. But the more I tried to shake her free, the more determined she was to hang on.

Have you ever tried to climb down a tree with a squirrel hanging from your hand, her teeth buried to the gums in your flesh, thinking you're going to die, screaming your head off, begging for someone to come to your rescue? Reminds me of the old adage "If a little kid who thinks he is going to die with a squirrel clamped on his hand and is screaming his lungs out and there is no one there to hear him, does he make a sound?"

Anyway, no one came to save the day, not even Mighty Mouse.

With my feet back on the ground, I grabbed the back of the squirrel's head and began squeezing. I didn't know what else to do, though I worried that if I killed her, then she'd die stuck to my hand and I'd never get her off. For a second I imagined what would happen if I had to make my way wearing a dead squirrel on my hand for the rest of my life. It would make shaking hands awkward, that's for sure.

When the squeezing didn't work, I changed my strategy, releasing her head and grabbing her by the tail with my other hand, then trying to pull her off. She still didn't let go, and soon she was stretched out straight from head to tail. I pulled harder. She bit harder. I pulled even harder. Finally, she let go and swung around in an attempt to bite my left hand. I let go of her tail, and, just like that, she hit the ground running.

Shaken up and with blood gushing down my arm, I headed home.

"Mom," I cried, opening the trailer door with a bang. "A squirrel bit me!"

Instead of pulling me into a great big hug and drying my tears, my mom grabbed her go-to disinfectant, a tincture of iodine, and got to work. The cure was worse, or at least equal to, the bite. Moral of the story? Never grab a wild squirrel by the tail!

BREAKING THE SPEED RECORD

After a few months living in the woods, my parents gave me a two-tone black-and-white pedal car, one of the coolest toys I ever received. There was a small hill near the end of the road, and sometimes I would push the car up to the top, get in, and coast down. The pedals gathered speed in equal measure to the rotation of the tires, and as the car's momentum increased, the pedals began to spin too fast for me to keep my feet on them. To avoid breaking a leg or two, I would hold my legs up in the air as I cruised down the hill. No one was around to see this, but I'm sure I made a strange sight.

The world's fastest pedal car.

One day, Mom must have been gazing out the window, saw me riding up and down the road, and thought she would give me the ride of my life. She was waiting for me outside as my little car approached the trailer.

"Herbie," she said, "you wanna go for a ride?" I nodded enthusiastically. She grabbed a rope and tied one end of it to the front of my pedal car and the other end to the back bumper of the Model A Ford. "Hold on tight!" she called as she pulled out onto the road.

Now, I can't tell you what in hell Mom was thinking. Looking back, this seems like a rather reckless way for a mother to behave. Maybe she was so focused on my having fun that she simply didn't consider one very important question: Once in motion, how would my little car stop?

Luckily, I knew to keep my feet up as the car accelerated. I do not know how fast we were going, but the pedals were spinning so fast that they were nothing but a blur. Dad, who'd been in the maintenance yard, must have heard the car and wondered what was going on. He ran out to the road, Mom slammed on the brake, and my little car, having no brakes whatsoever, kept on going, just missing the back of the Model A as it swung out to the side. The rope, when it stretched to its maximum length, yanked my little car around. A guardian angel must have been keeping an eye on me, because when the car flipped over, I'd cleared the hard-packed dirt road, landing in soft loamy soil that broke my fall. I lay there for a moment, dazed, then got up, a little scraped up but no worse for wear. If only someone had been recording it—I probably hold the world's speed record for a kid in a pedal car.

APPRENTICE LUMBERJACK

On one of my daily adventures, I came across a rafter of turkeys (that's what a group of turkeys is called; I looked it up) feeding in a small meadow. To a little boy with a lot of energy and not much impulse control, that bunch of turkeys existed for the sole purpose of being chased. I did not take into account that those big birds weren't much shorter than I was, those sharp grayish-brown beaks not too far below eye level—rarely did I take such potential dangers into account, even after that painful lesson from the squirrel. I just picked up a stick and off I went, running toward the rafter at full speed. Instead of giving me the pecking that I deserved, the turkeys scattered, scrambling for a short distance before taking flight. I kept chasing them as they flew off, leaving me, a lumbering wingless creature, behind. Once the last of their disapproving squawks faded away, I looked around.

The path and the area surrounding it didn't look familiar; somehow I'd managed to get farther from home than I ever had before. I turned around, studying the trees and the rocks and the angle of the sun for a clue. Then I heard a man's voice; it was not my dad's.

Thinking I was in big trouble, I turned in the direction of the voice, ready to make my excuses. There stood a couple of lumbermen sawing a tree with a two-man crosscut saw. Behind them their axes leaned against a log, with a couple of buckets on the ground next to them.

The man facing me must have heard my noisy run through the woods, and he was looking right at me. "Hey, kid," he yelled, "where did you come from? Are you lost?"

"No . . . not exactly," I said, keeping my distance as I was not totally sure about these two guys with the big axes. "I was running after the turkeys and then I watched them fly away. I live in the trailer."

"The one across from the maintenance yard?"

"Yeah."

The men kept working, and since they seemed friendly enough, I walked over.

"Hey," the lumberjack said, nodding to his companion. They put down the saw. Both took out their handkerchiefs to wipe the sweat from their faces. "Are you Howard Bryce's boy?"

"He's my dad."

"What's your name?"

"Herbie," I said.

"Hi, Herbie, I'm Bruce. This here is Darryl. Does your mom know where you are?"

"I . . . uh . . . She told me to go outside and play." My parents, to try to put a limit on my roaming territory, had told me not to cross any roads. Even though I'd complied, I realized now that my folks probably wouldn't be too happy with me. Fortunately, Bruce changed the subject.

"Ever see a big pine tree cut down?" he asked.

"I've seen mesquite trees cut down, but I've never seen a tree this big cut down."

"I'm going to let you help, but you will have to do everything I tell you and do it when I tell you. This is very dangerous, understand? We do not want the tree to fall on you, so you need to do what we say so you'll be safe."

"OK."

"Promise?"

"Promise."

While Bruce was picking up a couple of small dead branches, he called over to the other lumberjack. "Darryl, put the wedges in while I take care of the kid."

Bruce took his ax, cut the branches into four three-foot sticks, and made a square on the ground about twenty-five feet away from where they were working. "That's where you'll stand and watch. If you leave the square without my telling you, then you will have to go straight home. Understand?"

"I won't never get out unless you tell me to," I said, determined to witness the cutting down of this big pine tree.

"Come over here by the buckets." Bruce showed me a dishmop, which he called a brush, and a coffee can filled with oil that was inside one of the big buckets. "When we stop sawing and pound the wedges in, I'll ask you to come over and oil the saw for us. I'll show you how to put the oil on the saw the first time, and when you're done, you will go back and stand in your square. The next time we stop sawing and I ask you to oil the saw, come over and do it, then go back and stand in your square. Can you do that?"

"Yes," I said. I was getting excited. Wow! I was going to help cut down the tree.

Darryl called out, "Bruce, are we going to cut down this tree or are you going to talk with the kid all morning?"

"Hold your horses, Darryl. We've cut halfway through the tree already. We can't stop to take the kid home and just leave it. And the last thing we need is a kid running around in the woods while we're felling trees. If a tree falls on him, you and I will be looking for another job. If he's standing in that square, then at least we know where he is."

"All right, fine. But why in hell did you tell him he can oil the saw?"

"Come on, you have kids. Do you think he would stand in a square long enough for us to finish cutting this tree down? My boy sure wouldn't. It'll be faster and a lot safer this way, and when we're done one of us can take the kid home while the other delimbs the tree."

"Yeah, I guess you're right. Show the kid how to oil the saw, and let's get going. I'm about through with the wedges."

"OK, Herbie, come over here and put some oil on the saw."

The saw was still buried in the tree trunk, with Darryl's handle sticking out a few inches. Bruce dipped the brush in the can of oil, shook it off, and walked over to the saw. "Now watch here, Herbie. You start next to the tree and drag the brush along the saw, almost to the handle." He demonstrated, then dipped the brush into the oil again, shook it off, and handed it to me. Darryl pushed the saw back so that the blade was exposed on the other side of the tree. "Now you do this side of the saw."

I imitated his movements very carefully. When I was finished, I said, "Did I do it right?"

"Yeah, you did good. Now go stand in your square."

I ran over to the square and jumped inside, thrilled with my accomplishment. I heard the saw cutting through the trunk before I'd turned around. I stood there watching, waiting for the signal that they needed me to oil the saw. When they paused, I shouted, "Do you want me to oil the saw?"

"OK, Herbie, get over here and get this saw oiled." Bruce took the oil brush out, shook it off, and handed it to me. I did the first side, he dipped the brush in the oil again and handed it back to me, then I did the other side. When I finished, I rushed back to my square.

This is more fun than chasing turkeys! I thought. *I am helping cut down a big tree!*

A few seconds later, the men stopped sawing and switched to hammering the wedges. Then Darryl said, "Herbie, time to oil the saw."

I ran over as fast as I could, oiled the saw, ran back, and jumped in the square. A little more sawing, then a lot of pounding on the wedges, with Bruce pounding one and Darryl pounding the other. Then Bruce turned to me and yelled, "Stay there and don't move!"

After a couple more pounds on the wedges, there was a loud cracking sound. Darryl grabbed the saw and ran to the left, taking it with him. Bruce ran to the right, yelling, "TIMMBERRrrr! TIMMBERRrrr!" The cracking sound got louder and louder as the tree tipped. It paused for a moment as it came loose from the stump, then fell all the way to the ground with a fantastic thud that shook the forest floor. A flock of birds took flight, chirping in protest. Then it was silent.

Darryl grabbed the double-bladed ax and headed to the tree to begin the process of delimbing.

Bruce came over to my square, reached into his pocket, took out a nickel, and handed it to me. "That's what you earned for oiling our saw today. You did a good job. It's time I take you home now."

"Can I come back and do it again tomorrow?"

"Sorry, Herbie, you have to wait till you're all grown up and have graduated from high school before you can be a lumberjack."

"But you just said I did a good job."

"You did, but the boss wouldn't allow it. It is very, very dangerous work, too dangerous for a little boy."

I tried to hide my disappointment. Then I remembered that the adventures of the day were far from over—pretty soon I'd have to face my mom.

Bruce walked me home through the forest. I kept up with his steady pace, even though I wished we could slow down and delay the inevitable. Soon enough, I began to recognize the familiar landmarks of "my" forest.

I expected Mom to somehow already know that I had been in off-limits territory and to answer the door with the pancake turner, her favorite instrument of punishment, in her hand. Of course, she would have had no idea of my whereabouts, and so she looked surprised when she answered the door and saw me standing next to a sweaty, dusty lumberjack. "Ma'am," Bruce said, tipping his hat.

"Who are you, and what are you doing here with my son?" she asked.

Bruce introduced himself, then gave her the synopsis, her open-eyed look of surprise turning into a frown.

"Don't worry," he said, noting her mood. "We made sure your son was safe and sound at all times. He was a very good boy and did what he was told." Bruce then walked over to the maintenance yard to talk to Dad.

At supper that night, my part of the forest got a little smaller. While Mom was washing the dishes, Dad and I went out. "Stand here," he said, at the foot of the stairs coming down from the door. "From now on, you must be able to see the trailer from wherever you go. Am I making myself clear?"

"Yes, Dad," I said.

"All right, come with me." We walked over to a small tree near our front door. There, at the base of the trunk, was an iron metal triangle with a foot-long iron bar on a chain, which Dad had made after his little discussion with Bruce. "We're going to hang this up here," he said, knowing that if I "helped" in the process—just as I'd "helped" cut down the tree—I'd pay more attention.

After we finished hanging the iron triangle, Dad grabbed the iron bar and ran it around the inside of the triangle, making a loud ringing noise. Looking me straight in the eye, he said, "When you hear that sound, you stop what you're doing and come running home. You will *respond no matter what*."

Mom poked her head out the door, her face still flushed from washing the dishes. "Does it have to be so loud?"

"Yes, Louise, it does. I want Herbie to be able to hear it no matter where he is." Dad turned to me. "And what will you do when you hear it?" he said.

"I will come running home," I replied.

HERE COMES TROUBLE

That summer, my dad's youngest brother, Ed, came to stay with us. There was a nearly twenty-two-year gap between him and my dad, the oldest of the bunch, and Ed was more like my big brother, at only a year and a half older than me. I was excited—now I would have someone to play with.

One bright day, Ed and I crossed our road and wandered into the maintenance yard. It must have been the weekend, because it was quiet, the equipment still, like big sleeping metal beasts.

Now, I will not divulge the identity of the boy who first climbed the long loader crane, even though it's been more than eighty years. Let's just say that both Ed and I knew that playing on the log-loader crane was a double no-no, and that we both decided we were going to do it anyway.

As kids do, we played pretend, loading imaginary logs onto a nearby truck. It was like playing one of those claw crane arcade games, where you try to pick up a stuffed bear or a key chain and drop it in the slot, except that the claw was big enough to pick up giant logs, the arm was twenty-five feet long, the whole contraption probably weighed four or five thousand pounds, and the levers in front of the operator's chair weren't imaginary, not one bit.

So there we were, imagining pulling and pushing the levers, imagining the arm swinging around, imagining the claw clenching and unclenching. I'll admit, it was a ton of fun. That is, until one of us actually pulled on one of the levers, which released the cable brake. The cable, attached to its overhaul ball, started unrolling at a rapid speed. It dropped fast, and the overhaul ball landed on one of the log tongs, breaking it.

Uh-oh, I thought. I looked at Ed, and he looked at me. To the question of which one of us had pulled the cable release lever, I'll again claim the fifth. We both knew we were in deep doo-doo, and that both of us were going to catch hell when Dad found out.

Back at the trailer, we told Dad about the cable together, somehow omitting the fact of the broken tong from our confession. "Let's go take a look and see if there is any damage," he said, grabbing each of us by an arm.

We marched to the maintenance yard in silence. Right away he saw the cable undone, lying in a pile on the ground. "You two, stand here and think about what you did wrong while I start the engine and rewind the cable," Dad said. He walked over to the log-loading crane and climbed into the chair, then inserted a key into the ignition, pulled out the choke and throttle, stepped down and in front of the engine, grabbed the crank handle, and gave it a big twist. Nothing happened. He gave the crank another spin, which resulted in a few sputters. Third time was the charm; the engine kicked in and started running with a loud *tat-tat-tat*. Dad pushed the choke in and adjusted the throttle. The engine began to run more smoothly, and he returned to the operator's seat. He reached for a lever, gave it a little pull, and the cable started slowly winding back up.

I waited with bated breath. Maybe he wouldn't see the damage. Maybe, magically, the tong had somehow healed itself, like a broken finger or a squirrel bite does if you give it enough time. Maybe cows jump over the moon.

The cable stretched long, and the log-lifting tongs came off the ground. Of course, Dad noticed the broken tong. He pushed the lever back to stop the winding and set the cable brake, then jumped off the crane, walked over, and lifted the broken piece so he could take a nice long look. He turned it over and back, examining it from all sides, taking his time.

Then it happened. He released the tong, then unbuckled his belt and slowly took it off, something that I had, in my four and a half years on Earth, never seen him do before. His standard method of discipline was to say "Herb"—not the usual diminutive "Herbie"—to let me know that he was not pleased with whatever I had done. Then he'd say, "Do you want me to show you how to kick the crap out of a monkey and use you for the monkey?" followed by a tap on my butt with the side of his shoe. That little ritual, with its humor and gentleness, was effective because it was a wake-up call, a call for me to take inventory of who I was, what I was doing, and what I needed to do to correct the situation. I always got a kick out of it, too (pun intended), and it made me want to make my dad proud. (The last time he did it I was forty-eight years old, and it was still as funny as it was the first time.) I respected no one more than Dad, and I would do anything to get back in his good graces.

Now, Dad made his way toward us unhurriedly; we both knew what was coming.

"You trying to get me fired?" he said, his voice dangerously soft. "Why were you over here? You know you're not allowed to be over here unless I bring you over here. Now, both of you, turn around."

We did as we were told. Dad waited a moment, allowing time for our nervousness to grow. A cold sweat gathered at the base of my spine.

Whack! Dad gave me a swat on the behind; I did my best not to cry out. If you've never been hit on the bum with a belt, I can tell you that even a gentle swat hurts like hell. *Whack!* One swat for Ed. *Whack! Whack! Whack! Whack!*

We each received three swats, and I kept my eyes closed tightly, waiting for swat number four. Instead of delivering another whack, Dad said, "Go on home." He sounded more sad than mad, which made me feel even worse.

As Ed and I ran, I looked back over my shoulder; Dad had put his belt back on and was carrying the broken tong toward the welding machine.

That was the first and only time Dad ever gave me a spanking. The drama of his removing his belt and his stern yet calm voice was more effective than the three swats themselves. I will never forget it, not because of the spanking but because I knew the rules, I had accepted them, and my dad had trusted me and given me the freedom to be myself. And I had let him down.

As the dry, exhausted heat of summer signaled the season's end, Ed moved back to Oak Creek Canyon to live with his sister Beulah and her husband, Colbert Boutwell. I was sad to see him go but knew that he was going to a more entertaining place—Oak Creek Canyon had a large creek full of trout to catch, pools to swim in and skip rocks across, a waterfall with a rock shaped like a water slide to slide down, and big boulders to climb. And Beulah and Colbert owned the Indian Gardens skating rink. It was a little boy's heaven.

GRANDPA AND GRANDMA, MOVE OVER, HERE WE COME

I heard the triangle ringing, and so I raced home. When I got there, I found Mom and Dad loading up the car. The rumble seat was open, and they were running back and forth between the car and the trailer, grabbing whatever they could from inside and stuffing it into the car.

"Get in!" Dad yelled. I was confused but didn't hesitate, jumping in with him and Mom right after me. Once the three of us were in the car, Dad put the pedal to the metal, pulling onto the main logging road with a spewing of gravel and a cloud of dust, heading at full speed north toward Mormon Lake. Then I saw why we were in such a hurry: the forest was on fire. That is the last image I remember about my summer in the forest—a sky gray with smoke, the crackling sound of burning timber, the feeling of drawing hot ash into my lungs with every breath.

Everything that my parents hadn't been able to pack into the car went up in flames. Mom was three months pregnant and wanting to be near her mother when the baby was born, so we headed to Grandpa and Grandma's farm to start over again.

Once we were out of danger, we settled into the two-hundred-mile drive. I was excited to go back to the farm I loved, to go home.

When we pulled up, Grandpa was plowing the field, and Maxine and Falene were helping Grandma in the garden. Talmage and Callis were nowhere to be seen. Of course, there were no cell phones in those days, so we hadn't called ahead, and they were plenty surprised by our sudden arrival, though I'm sure my parents and grandparents had been hatching a plan for the arrival of the baby.

"Well, hello!" my grandma said, patting my back as I clung to her legs, overjoyed to be Grandma's little boy again.

Grandma was starting to can the summer harvest so we'd have a supply of food for the winter, and she was happy to get extra help in the kitchen. She'd already canned some fruits, tomatoes, and root vegetables, and made jams, jellies, sauces, catsup, and pickles, the jars lined up in their usual spot in the cellar, along with apple-box crates of potatoes, yams, onions, garlic, pumpkins, winter squash, apples, and the five-gallon crock of Grandpa's sauerkraut he made every fall. The winter garden still had more root vegetables, greens, peas, beans, and corn ready to be canned.

I loved helping Grandma and Mom harvest the pinto beans, butter beans, and black-eyed peas. We picked the bean pods, and then laid them out on a canvas tarp in the sun to dry. Mom and Grandma gossiped while shelling the beans once they dried, and stored them in cotton flour sacks, all from the comfort of chairs under the shady cottonwood tree. Grandma and Grandpa had instated the southern tradition of eating black-eyed peas and greens on New Year's Day to bring good luck and prosperity in the upcoming year. I, for one, always thought I had good luck if I could talk my way out of eating them. To me they tasted like what I guessed dirt would taste like. Yuck!

While the female side of the family was busy canning, the male side was responsible for plowing the fields in preparation for planting the fall crops. This division of labor was absolutely essential to the survival of the family, and every person's efforts counted. Though my uncles Talmage and Callis and the hired farmhands were good workers, Grandpa was glad to have my dad's help, too.

To keep the dairy farm in operation, the cows needed to give birth to a calf every year so that they would keep producing milk. A couple of days after the calves were born, my grandpa and uncles would have to separate them from their mothers and, if they were male, decide what to do with them. There were no decisions to be made for the female calves—each would have the vital job of producing milk once she was grown. The male calves, on the other hand, were more expendable. For them, there were three options: first, get eaten; second, get sold; third, let them keep their testicles and raise them for breeding. I'm sure all the male calves would've preferred the last option, but only one bull is required per herd, so not many get to realize that dream.

Along with the steers—the male cows who'd been castrated—that would supply our beef, we raised a few turkeys, ducks, several chickens, and pigs. We ate the turkeys, roasted and stuffed, during the holidays. The roasted stuffed ducks were saved for company and, because duck meat was his favorite, Grandpa's birthday. Chickens provided eggs and the meat for stews, soup, dumplings, and the family's universal favorite, fried chicken.

As for the pigs, we used the whole animal to make bacon, ham, pork belly, ham hocks, ribs, sausage, pork rinds . . . the list goes on. The average-size pig, at about 250 pounds, will render twenty to thirty pounds of lard, an essential and versatile cooking staple. All that lard makes a lot of piecrusts, as well as candles and soap.

When the butchering was done and the various meats were prepped and ready to be smoked, they were taken to Uncle Van's smokehouse, which was shared by the community. It was a round building with a thatched roof that had a hole for a chimney at its peak. I remember walking through and looking up in amazement at the dozens of hams, slabs of bacon, fleshy ham hocks, and countless strings of sausages hanging from the ceiling. All were continuously bathed in smoke, which came from the large fire pit in the middle of the room. Small mesquite logs burned down slowly, forming a thick layer of dusty white-hot embers. The fee for using the smokehouse was enough mesquite logs to replenish and add to the woodpile; that's it. Though the process was labor intensive, the taste was well worth it. Yum!

As I mentioned, we had plenty of cows to supply our meat, as well as our milk. What about cheese, cottage cheese, sour cream, and butter? Once the cows had made their contribution, Grandma took over. All of us helped out, in particular for butter churning, which was a family affair. Grandma would fill the churn or churns about two-thirds full of heavy cream that had been "ripened" by sitting on the counter at room temperature all day. This allowed for the necessary bacteria to grow.

After supper, while my aunts Falene and Maxine washed the dishes, the rest of us sat around the table taking turns cranking the butter churns. For best results, you need to get a rhythm going, and it takes about thirty minutes of churning to form the butter. I always got to start, because after five or ten turns of the crank, I'd be about ready for a nap. Then Grandma would relieve me, turning that crank with what looked like ease; my grandma had had a lifetime to build up her butter-making muscles. After everyone took their turn and she was satisfied with the consistency, Grandma lined the inside of a colander with cheesecloth, then poured the contents of the churn into the colander to separate the buttermilk from the butter. (Grandpa always got the first glass of the buttermilk.) Next, she rinsed the butter until it was free of buttermilk and put it in a bowl. To rid it of any last remaining liquid, she would take a wooden spoon and press all of the water out, then add salt to taste, and shape it. She used a butter mold to shape it when company was coming for dinner and holidays; otherwise, a hunk of butter worked just fine.

Last but not least: deer. Venison is a much leaner meat than beef and perfect for jerky. After the venison was thinly sliced and seasoned in brine with spices, it was hung on a clothesline and covered with cheesecloth to keep flies and wasps off. After it was dried, it was stored in cotton bags hung on a peg behind the woodstove, providing the family with quick, tasty protein all winter. (After growing up on real jerky, I always have to say "No, thanks" when offered the store-bought kind. It's just not the same.)

But, before we could start making that jerky, the deer had to be hunted first.

AIM AT THE DEER, NOT YOUR THUMB!

A couple of months after moving in with Grandpa and Grandma, my dad, his brother Ebbie, and a couple of friends went deer hunting on horseback up on Mount Graham. I wasn't there, obviously, because I was too young. But I do remember Dad riding off, his wide-brim hat blocking the morning sun. And I certainly remember his dramatic return.

Here's how the story goes: After setting up camp, the group roped off an area nearby to create a makeshift corral for the horses and lined up their saddles, with the rifle scabbards still attached, on a log next to it. The next morning, as the sun peeked over the horizon, the four men set out on foot to hunt for deer. They didn't have much luck, and they returned empty-handed, tired, and parched.

The first thing Dad did when he got back to camp, before he took a drink of water or sat down to rest, was to walk over to his saddle to put his rifle away in his scabbard. This is when the comedy—or tragedy, depending on who was telling the story—of errors really began.

Error #1: One of the other guys had put their gun in Dad's scabbard.

Error #2: The gun was upside down, with the barrel sticking out.

Error #3: The rifle had a bullet in the chamber. This oversight was so egregious that checking for it never even crossed Dad's mind. No one with more than a couple of brain cells to rub together would have put a still-loaded gun away—or so Dad assumed.

Error #4, the biggest error of them all: When taking ahold of the rifle to pull it out of the scabbard, Dad put the base of his thumb over the end of the barrel. You know, where the bullet comes out. He pulled on the rifle; it didn't move. He pulled a little harder, the rifle moved a bit, but it was still stuck. Third try's a charm, and a big yank freed the rifle from the scabbard. Unfortunately, it also freed Dad's thumb from his hand.

As the rifle came out, the firing hammer got pulled back, then, once clear of the scabbard, it sprang back with enough force to fire the gun. *Boom!* Dad saw it before he felt it: there was his thumb, dangling from his hand, blood spraying into the dust. The other men came running, saw Dad on his knees, his left hand cradling his right. "My . . . my thumb," he said, white in the face.

They quickly wrapped Dad's hand in as clean a cloth as they could find, careful to protect the little strip of flesh that was keeping the thumb attached. Ebbie helped him get on his horse, then climbed up on his own, and together the two of them headed to the hospital in Safford, located about fifteen miles away. Can you imagine trying to ride a horse with your thumb hanging on by a thread?

Remember, this was 1938, dozens of years before the first surgical reattachment of a digit. Cocaine was the primary anesthesia of the day, and perhaps my dad got himself a sniff. No one there would have had whiskey to offer to help numb the pain, so my guess is that Dad had to suffer through a very long night.

All my dad's and his brother's efforts to preserve the thumb turned out to be moot; with a snip of the surgical scissors, off it came. The doctor cleaned the wound, sewed up the area where Dad's thumb used to be, and called it a day.

Dad spent a couple of days in the hospital for observation. After a few hours, when he'd had time to recover from the shock, he asked what they had done with his thumb, and the answer he got was "We buried it in the flower garden." I remember overhearing Dad tell this story and wanting to know if someone had made a thumb-size coffin for it before the burial, then wondering about what might have happened if a gardener accidentally dug it up.

In terms of firsthand memory, that's pretty much it. Except for one other surreal scene: I'm in a dark room, the only light coming from a coal oil lamp on the table. I'm sitting in a chair with my elbows on the table, my chin resting in my hands, watching Dad use the handle of a wooden spoon to stuff cotton into the thumb of a leather glove.

For a while after the accident, Dad was very self-conscious about his missing appendage, and he did his best to hide this lack. The fact that the thumb was missing from his right hand made it even harder. Even when he wore a glove stuffed with cotton, all it took was a handshake to give him away. Once his hand healed, he gave up the glove, but he still kept his hand in his pocket when out in public. Of course, this drew more attention than it would've otherwise. Eventually, Dad got used to it, and once he stopped noticing it, so did other people. It wasn't a handicap, and I don't recall it interfering with his life in any significant way.

Decades later, I was teasing one of my young sons about him sucking his thumb.

"If you keep it up," I said, "you'll suck this thumb right off, just like your grandpa did!"

His mother, rightly so, said, "Stop telling him things like that."

"How do you think my dad lost his thumb?" I asked.

"Your dad isn't missing a thumb." She had known my dad for over eight years at this point.

"Yes, he is. He doesn't have a thumb on his right hand. He shot it off when I was five years old, and I can assure you it did not grow back."

"C'mon, I know he isn't missing a thumb."

"Check it out the next time you see him."

The next time she saw her father-in-law and discovered that I had been telling the truth, she was so surprised that she said, "You are missing a thumb!"

Totally deadpan, Dad replied, "Yeah, I sucked my thumb off when I was a little boy."

She turned to me and said, "You told him to say that."

Laughing, I said, "No, I didn't, but I was hoping he would. I've heard him telling that to people, especially kids, many times." I'll bet it has curbed at least a couple of kids' thumb-sucking habit, too.

GOODBYE, ASHURST. HELLO, TEMPE.

Two and a half months later, my sister Patsy entered my life. It was a complicated birth, and my parents returned to Safford Hospital to have the baby.

I was excited to be the big brother of a new baby sister. No longer would I be the youngest, and now *I* had someone to boss around just like my aunts and uncles bossed me.

Shortly thereafter, we were on the move again. This time, it wasn't just Mom, Dad, and me; of course, baby Patsy was coming along, as were Grandpa, Grandma, Talmage, Callis, Falene, and Maxine.

Grandma's mother, Mary Mashburn, was living in Georgia and had become very ill. Her doctor recommended that she move to a drier climate, and Irene, Grandma's eldest daughter, volunteered to have my great-grandmother move in with her and her family in Tempe, just east of Arizona State Teachers College. (The name of this institution would be changed to Arizona State College in 1945, and finally to Arizona State University in 1958.)

Irene and her husband, Milton, were very active in the Mormon Church and close friends with Marlon Turley, their bishop. A bishop is the leader of a local congregation (known as a ward), and he—it's always a man—has duties similar to those of a pastor, priest, or rabbi. This position is unpaid, and so most bishops have their own careers in addition to serving the church.

Bishop Turley's career was in farming, including pig farming. He owned several hundred acres of land. The price of pork was rising fast, and all reports suggested that it would continue to climb, so he'd purchased several hundred pigs and turned eighty acres of his land into a pig farm. In a conversation with Milton and Irene, Turley mentioned that he needed someone to run the farm and asked if they knew anyone. They recommended Dad. Turley called Dad and invited him down to talk about running the farm.

So while Grandma was staying with Irene to help care for her mother, Dad agreed to run the pig farm, and Grandpa rented eighty acres from Turley until he could sell the farm in Ashurst and find one to buy in the Tempe/Mesa area. And so began our year of the pigs.

CHAPTER 4

The Pig Farm: 1939–1940

Dad turned our 1930 Model A Ford Coupe off Apache Trail Road onto the narrow dirt road leading to the center of activity on Bishop Turley's pig farm. There they were: pigs, pigs, pigs everywhere, as far as my five-year-old eyes could see. A gazillion pigs, at least—I'd never seen so many pigs in my life.

"Want to see some pigs and their little piglets?" Dad had said to me that morning, thinking that I might enjoy such a sight. Boy, was he ever right. I was fascinated by the whole thing: the squealing, the snorting, the big leathery noses twitching in the air. Gestation takes approximately 116 days, so it is possible for a sow to have two to three litters per year, with ten to twelve piglets per litter, meaning there were pigs of all ages, from teeny-tiny babies with the cutest little ears imaginable to great big bristly mom and dad pigs of up to 250 pounds, brown ones and gray ones and white ones and spotted ones and, of course, ones that were the quintessential piggy pink.

Marlon W. Turley was the first man to serve as bishop of the local Tempe Mormon ward, created in 1928. I only ever heard him referred to as Bishop Turley (in fact, I only learned his first name when I googled him while writing this book). He had the biggest pig farm in the area and had invited my dad down to talk about running the farm. Many years later, Dad told me that the farm didn't have a gazillion pigs—more like five hundred. That's still an awful lot of pigs.

Dad and I got out of the car and headed toward some pens containing droves of weaned pigs. My dad put his hand up to his face to block the sun, then scanned the area, looking around for Bishop Turley.

"Howard," a deep voice called out, "over here, in the shade." Dad headed over to a tree by the fence for what would turn out to be a shocking conversation. I followed close at his heels, curious about what kind of man could be the boss of so many pigs.

Turley was a stocky man in his late fifties or early sixties, with a slight root-beer belly (not a beer belly—he was a Mormon bishop, after all) and a smile both on his lips and in his eyes. He held one boot in his hand, looking as though he'd just been shaking out a rock that had gotten inside. When Dad approached, Bishop Turley shifted his boot to his left hand and offered his right hand to shake. Dad grabbed his hand, let out a "Damn!" and jumped back, then started laughing. Turley laughed, too. I stared at them, confused.

Turley hadn't taken his boot off to shake out a rock; he'd done it so he could place his sweaty sock-encased foot on an electric wire that ran about four inches above the ground, all the way around the entire property. It was meant to keep the pigs from rooting under the fence. Dad learned his lesson—and pulled the same prank many times later on.

While Dad and Turley talked, I ran around, poking my nose into everything per usual. Right away I noticed a big pile of bread, interspersed with a few cakes, pies, cupcakes, and donuts, still in their wrapping and boxes. "What's this?" I called out, forgetting my manners and interrupting the grown-ups.

"Twice a week, big trucks from Holsum and Rainbow bring old baked goods and dump them on the ground there," Bishop Turley told me. "We feed it to the pigs." In 1939, bakery outlet stores hadn't been invented yet, so this was a win-win situation for the bakeries and the pigs and, as I'd soon find out, for me.

"If I were a pig," I said, "I'd only eat the cupcakes and pies."

"Well, the workers get first dibs. Then they remove the wrappers and boxes and toss all the bread and pastries into tanks filled with whey."

"What's whey?" I asked, turning to my dad.

"You've seen your grandma pour that watery milk into buckets for the chickens or the pigs' slop?"

"Yeah."

"That's whey. When milk clabbers, curds are the solid, and whey is the watery stuff."

I couldn't understand how anyone, including pigs, would want to eat anything soaked in whey. Seeing me looking hungrily toward the pile, Bishop Turley said, "Why don't you go ahead and take some cupcakes? I thought I saw a chocolate cake, too—I bet your mama would like to have it for dessert tonight."

A BIG MUD PUDDLE

Part of the agreement that Dad and Bishop Turley struck was that Dad would build a small house on the farm with the help of the hired hands. This was a good deal for Dad—Bishop Turley would pay for the labor, and the mud was free.

The soil about eighteen inches below the surface was perfect for making the adobe bricks, each of which was four inches high, eight inches wide, and sixteen inches long. These big bricks would provide great insulation, keeping the house cool in summer and warm in winter. Digging a hole for the sandy clay or loamy soil had the added benefit of creating a small root cellar.

Dad and his crew let me help by throwing straw into the mud to make the mortar to bind the bricks together. "Herbie," my dad said, a serious look on his face, "your job is the most important, because the straw is what holds the mud together and keeps the bricks from cracking or breaking. We can't let the bricks break and fall apart, or the house will fall down. Can you handle such an important job?"

"Yes, Dad," I said, trying to look humble.

Upon reflection, I've come to see that Dad was setting it up so that I wouldn't try to mess about in the pit full of mud, just as those lumberjacks had let me "help" them by oiling the saw and therefore ensuring that I wouldn't get underfoot. Oh, but how I wanted to get down in the mud and stomp around like the men were doing. Can you imagine how much fun a five-year-old boy could have in all that mud? There are few sounds in this world more satisfying than the squelch of a bare foot forcefully applied to a wet pat of mud, or few feelings better than that of cool mud oozing between your toes or splashed on your face. But, alas, my job was too important; I was needed to throw straw into the mud. It was up to me to make the house strong and safe, a heavy responsibility but one that I shouldered with the appropriate solemnity.

I knew I was growing up fast because I had the most important job there was when making adobes, and I got to help tear off the bread wrappers and open the pastry boxes and put the bread and pastries in the whey tanks, and the paper and cardboard in the burn barrels. Plus I got shocked a couple of times on the electric fence and didn't even die! And soon I would be going to school.

HOUSE OF SCORPIONS

While waiting for the adobe house to be completed, we moved into a very small one-bedroom house on the south bank of the Salt River, near where Arizona State University's Sun Devil Stadium stands today. Before you start picturing some idyllic cottage with a green lawn leading down to the edge of the river, maybe a small dock with a little canoe gently rocking in the breeze, let me set the record straight. This was 1939, and Arizona had yet to recover from the Great Depression, so, generally speaking, most parts of the state, and particularly rural areas, were on the underdeveloped side. Perhaps the word "house" is euphemistic, maybe even an outright exaggeration. There was no grass, no boat, and no dock from which to launch, nor water to float in. Just lots of sand and river rocks and a high white sun and some thirsty vegetation poking out here and there—the Salt River was an arroyo, a dry riverbed that hadn't seen water, except for an occasional flash flood after a large rainstorm, since Granite Reef Diversion Dam had been completed in 1908.

What the area lacked in water, however, it made up for in scorpions. Specifically, Arizona bark scorpions, three-inch-long yellow demons that are the most venomous scorpions in North America. Not only does their sting hurt like hell and induce numbness and vomiting that can last up to three days, it can kill smaller creatures like—you guessed it—small children and babies. And unlike other kinds of scorpions, which tend to go solo, Arizona bark scorpions are a friendlier bunch, gathering in groups by the dozen. They like to congregate, and our house, far from being new, had lots of little nooks and crannies through which the scorpions could enter. And enter they did, gathering at night to look for food. Even now, just thinking about them gives me the willies.

My small bed was at the foot of my parents' bed, and Patsy's bassinet was on Mom's side of the bed, in easy reach for middle-of-the-night feedings. When we first moved in, Mom and Dad had placed the feet of our bed frames and bassinet in cans filled with water so that the scorpions couldn't climb up and get into our beds. I wasn't allowed to get out of bed or put my shoes on until an adult had inspected the floor and the insides of my shoes.

One night, I was awakened by my dad yelling, "Damn it, woman, stop hitting me with that damn flashlight! Stop, stop it! You're going to break every bone in my back!"

I looked over to see Mom hysterically screaming and beating Dad's back with a flashlight. Later they'd explain that Dad had been awakened by a scorpion stinging his back.

"Louise," he'd whispered, trying not to wake me and the baby or provoke the already provoked arachnid, "I just got stung by a scorpion, and I can feel it crawling underneath my undershirt. Go slow now . . . take the flashlight and see if you can find it."

Now, imagine that it's the dead of night and your bed-mate has just been stung by a scorpion determined enough to overcome the obstacle of cans full of water, and there's plenty more where that one came from, perhaps crawling on the ceiling above at that very moment, and you also have a quite reasonable terror of scorpions, and your young son and newborn are just a couple of feet away. Would you keep your cool?

My mom certainly did not keep hers. When she saw the scorpion, her mama-bear survival instinct kicked into overdrive. She would kill the little monster no matter what and with the closest weapon available, which happened to be that same flashlight in her hand. She set about ending it once and for all, but it's hard to see your target when you're swinging the only light in the room with each and every blow. I remember glimpses of the scene as the light briefly illuminated it: Mom's face, twisted in fear; a circle of ceiling, edged by darkness; Dad's hunched back, his hands protecting the base of his skull. My sister woke up and started crying. My mom screamed and hit. My dad pleaded for her to stop. It was utter chaos. I assume that my mom's strategy was: *If I strike often enough, I'm bound to hit the scorpion eventually.*

Mom stopped only when she was sure that she'd mashed the scorpion into pulp. She eased it, with Dad's shirt, up and over his head. "Go throw this in the burn pile," she told her bruised and stung husband. From then on, I sure hoped Mom wouldn't find a scorpion on me.

A-HUNTING WE WILL GO

To supplement our food budget, Dad hunted for quails, doves, and cottontail rabbits, which were abundant along the dry river bottom. He usually took me along. Walking along the arroyo provided good father-son bonding time, as well as an opportunity to teach me how to safely handle a gun.

He considered it his job to dress out the game. I won't go into too much bloody detail here, but essentially this means peeling off the skin, removing the innards, and cutting the animal up into pieces that are easy to prepare and cook. Obviously, this involves a strong stomach—and a really sharp knife.

After one of our rabbit-hunting trips, we were late getting home with our bounty. Dad left the two rabbits on a table at the side of the house, designated for just this purpose. "Stay put," he said to me, "and keep an eye on the rabbits while I get my boning knife." He opened the front door to find Mom standing there, dressed and ready to go.

"It's Wednesday," she said. "MIA starts in thirty minutes. You better get a move on."

MIA, which stands for Mutual Improvement Association, was a program for twelve- to eighteen-year-old members of the Church of the Latter-day Saints. Mom taught the MIA Maids, while Dad assisted the local Boy Scouts troop.

"I need to dress out the rabbits now or we'll have to throw them away," Dad said.

"We don't have time for you to dress them out," Mom replied. "Get in the house and change into your Scout clothes." When she saw him pause, she continued, "I'll wrap them up in newspaper. They'll keep for a couple of hours." Then she turned to me. "Go on down to Grandpa and Grandma's. Tell them we'll drop Patsy off on our way."

I looked at my mother, then looked at the rabbits. "I can peel the rabbits and take out their guts, just like Daddy does. I've watched him do it lots of times."

Mom's response was sharp. "Don't you dare try dressing those rabbits while we're gone!" With that, she turned and went in the house to get Patsy. Calling back over her shoulder, she said, "Leave those rabbits be and get going."

Dad stepped out the door; he'd managed to change his clothes and even wash his hands and face.

"Daddy," I said, appealing to parent number two, "I can clean the rabbits while you're at church."

"No, Herbie, you're too young. You could cut yourself."

"I've watched you do it many times. I can do it!"

"Just leave them and get on down to your grandpa and grandma's like your mom said."

"Fine," I replied with a scowl.

Well, turns out I didn't quite make it down to my grandparents' house. Those rabbits needed to be dressed out, and, by gum, I was just the boy to do it! I headed down the road as instructed, but as soon as the car drove out of sight, I turned around and, once home, got Dad's boning knife down from the kitchen counter where he'd left it. I was tall enough by this point to reach the counter, which, in my opinion, meant I was tall enough for the task at hand.

Outside, I unwrapped the rabbits and sat down with them on the floor of the porch. They were no longer warm but still fluffy and soft. Some way or another, I got those two rabbits skinned, their feet, tails, and heads off, and their guts removed. Then I took the rabbits into the house, washed them, wrapped them in wax paper, and put them in the icebox. I did not cut myself, not even once, not even a teeny-tiny nick.

I waited impatiently for Mom and Dad to get home, listening for their car on the road. Finally, I heard the sound of gravel crunching under rolling tires, and I stood up and ran down the front steps, hardly waiting for them to get out before telling them what I'd done.

But instead of the praise I was foolishly expecting, I got two scoldings at the same time. "You could have cut your hand off! You might've landed yourself in the hospital or maybe even killed yourself!" Mom said, while simultaneously Dad said, "You are not old enough. I need to teach you the right way first!"

My answer? "But look! No cuts." I showed them my hands, front and back, to prove it. "And I did it right, I promise. Go to the icebox and see."

My parents looked at each other, communicating without words in the way that parents do. They made their way over, opened the door, and took out the rabbits. A bit of blood had soaked through the wax paper, but otherwise everything was neat and tidy.

I think Dad was impressed, but he wouldn't show it, because he did not want to encourage me to do such a dangerous thing again on my own or to disobey direct orders. I'll bet he was counting his lucky stars, too, that he hadn't walked in to find me passed out in a pool of my own blood, two dead rabbits on the ground beside me. On top of that, I'm sure he was planning to approach the teaching process as a master to an apprentice, handing down the knowledge his own father taught to him, when he thought I was old enough, which would have been many more years down the road. Perhaps he regretted my growing up so fast.

I do know for a fact, however, that Mom was impressed. She was overheard by a reporter expressing as much to a neighbor, and the story of my successful dressing out was published in the local newspaper.

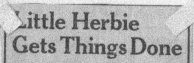

Little Herbie Gets Things Done

Little five year old Herbie Brice is a big help to his mother; in fact in an emergency Herbie could probably run the household.

While Mrs. Howard Brice was in the home of a neighbor, taking care of a member of their family who was ill, Mr. Brice killed two rabbits and then discovered that neither he nor Mrs. Brice had time to clean them before they spoiled. Herbie, overhearing the discussion, informed his parents that he knew how to clean rabbits and he would not mind the job at all.

Both parents, immediately forbade him to touch the rabbits, but Herbie decided that it was time to take matters into his own hands. In no time at all he had both rabbits "peeled" and put away in the refrigerator, against the time when he would feel the pangs of hunger, so familiar to five-year-olds.

Herbie's mother says that she couldn't have done a better job and that all she had to do was toss them into the pan.

TALMAGE'S REIGN OF TERROR BEGINS

A short time after our little midnight adventure with the scorpion, my mom's parents moved from their daughter

Irene's house to a rental farm about an eighth of a mile down the road, closer to town. After they were settled in, we moved in with them. Since I was only five years old, no one told me anything, so I'm not sure if the decision was made due to our scorpion problem or to save money. Probably both. At least Dad was safe—or, at least, safer—from another flashlight attack.

My aunts Maxine and Falene and uncles Talmage and Callis were also living with Grandpa and Grandma, making a total of ten living in the house. My parents, my sister, and I lived in part of a barn that had been converted to living quarters; the other part was used as a storage shed. The barn had a corrugated galvanized metal roof, and when it rained—and it rains hard in Arizona—it sounded like someone pouring marbles into a large metal bucket. The first time it hailed, I thought someone was shooting a machine gun at us. I got very little sleep on rainy nights and none at all when it hailed. But at least there were no more scorpions! Well, maybe one every now and then.

September was fast approaching, so it was time to enroll my aunts in elementary school and my uncles in high school. Grandma took me along even though I was still considered too young to go to school, since Arizona didn't have kindergarten at that time. She worked her charm, however, and so when we got home, we announced to my parents that Maxine was enrolled in the fourth grade, Falene in the seventh, Talmage at the high school as a senior, Callis as a junior, and I would begin first grade! My birthday was about ten weeks past the cutoff, but somehow Grandma got them to look the other way, and there I was, a big boy going to start at Tempe Grammar School in a few weeks.

We lived a little more than a mile from school, and I was going to get to walk to school with my aunts and uncles, stopping halfway to pick up a couple of cousins, Arvilla and Milton Jr. (we all called him Junior), both in high school. As it turned out, I mostly walked with the girls, as the guys didn't want to be seen with a first grader or their sisters. When the guys did pay attention to me, I should have smelled trouble, especially when it came to Talmage and Milton. Talmage, in particular, loved to play pranks. He hadn't been all that interested in me when I was a toddler down on Grandma and Grandpa's farm, but now that I was older, he seemed to go out of his way to harass me.

I got out of school earlier than Maxine, Falene, and Arvilla, and I was supposed to wait on the playground until they were released and we could walk home together. Classes started and ended by the ringing of a big bell in the bell tower, so why wait around when I could go on adventures, then hurry back at the sound of the bell? I'd become an expert at this system with the iron triangle at our house in the woods. Anyway, if I was a little late, I could just tell them that I was in the bathroom or something.

Arizona State Teachers College was across the street and to the east of the elementary school, and Tempe High School was across the street to the north, which gave me plenty of places to explore. An added bonus: the high school and college girls thought I was cute and made a big fuss over me.

While on one of my afternoon adventures wandering around the perimeter of the high school, Talmage saw me and called me over. "C'mon over here, Herbie," he said. I walked over and tilted my head to look up at my tall uncle, who, to a first grader, seemed like a grown-up. "I want to show you something," he said, taking an envelope out of his back pocket. I'd already learned basic reading, and I could read the letters M-R-S and my last name written on it. "This is a letter from Mrs. Theu to your mother."

Why would my teacher be writing to Mom? I wondered. Talmage explained: "Your teacher was looking all over for you and couldn't find you on the playground where you're supposed to be." He shook his head, clearly dismayed by my misbehavior, then handed me the letter. "Here, I think you should be the one to give it to her."

Now, if you had an uncle who played so many tricks on you that you referred to him as your "naughty uncle," wouldn't you see a big red flag waving in front of your face? But I was young and naïve, and the only thing I could think about was that I was going to be in big trouble.

On the way home, I walked next to my aunts with dread. What would my punishment be? A talking-to, a spanking with the pancake turner, something worse? What if Mom pulled me out of school? What if she pulled me out of school and never let me go back, not ever again?

By the time we got home, my feet felt like they were filled with sand, my arms made of lead. Under Talmage's watchful eye, I handed Mom the letter and watched with trepidation as she slowly, slowly, slowly opened the letter.

Dear Mrs. Bryce,

Herbie has been leaving the school grounds and smoking. I have seen him give cigarettes to two other boys. I think you need to talk with him and tell him he can't bring cigarettes to school. The school will not tolerate this kind of behaver in the future.

Concerned,
Mrs. Thew

First Grade teacher

Mom's head snapped up when she was finished reading, a look of shock and anger on her face. She grabbed me by the shoulder. "Go get the pancake turner!" she yelled. Just as I'd feared.

"Hold on a second," Grandma said, coming to the rescue. "Let me see that letter." She held out her hand. I watched her, waiting for the verdict. After reading it, she looked at me, then at my mom. "If Herbie had been smoking like this letter says he did, don't you think we would be able to smell it on his breath and clothing?"

Mom started sniffing the air around me like a dog searching for a bone. Satisfied, she said, "Well, I guess you're right." They both agreed that I passed the smell test. The next thing out of Grandma's mouth was "Louise, how does Herbie's teacher spell her name?"

"T-H-E-U," Mom replied.

"Take another look at this letter. Notice how Mrs. Theu's name is spelled here in the signature?"

Mom looked, her brow crinkling. "T-H-E-W . . . Who gave you this letter?" she said to me.

All kinds of thoughts started running through my head. *If I tell her that Talmage gave me the letter, she will know that I left school grounds and was over at the high school. If I* don't *tell her that Talmage gave me the letter, she might think that my teacher actually wrote it. "U" and "W" sort of look alike, after all. And then she'll believe that I had been smoking.*

I was boxed in on all sides; no matter what I said, I was going to be in trouble. Finally, I decided to deal with the devil I knew. "Talmage gave it to me," I blurted out.

Wow! Was it ever satisfying to see my five-foot-six-inch grandmother turn on my six-foot-tall uncle. To quote my mom, "She was on him like a duck on a June bug." Grandma looked Talmage straight in the eyes, then drawled those dreaded words: "Go-o-o fe-e-etch me-e a swi-i-itch!"

We all knew that tone. It meant that you'd better choose a switch big enough to mete out the punishment you deserved. Somehow, Grandma always seemed to live nearby a healthy old tree, with many different-size branches for the choosing. She knew what she was doing; the more you thought about it, the harder you were on yourself and the more you wished that you hadn't done whatever you did. It wasn't the swats that taught the lesson—it was the mental agony that you put yourself through.

Talmage, not wanting to stoke the fire of Grandma's wrath, didn't mention the fact of my being at the high school. I was glowing inside with satisfaction. Finally—finally!—Talmage was going to get his comeuppance for teasing and pulling pranks on me.

A LIFE LESSON AND THE ART OF PULLING PRANKS

Besides my little sister, who didn't count because she was just a baby, I was the youngest and, accordingly, the most gullible. This made me an easy target for Talmage's pranks, and I grew up wary of my uncle yet always falling for it. There wasn't much entertainment back then—electrical televisions had recently hit the marketplace, but they certainly hadn't made it to Tempe, Arizona—and so we made our own. I think that Talmage must have stayed awake at night thinking up pranks to pull on people. At least he wasn't discriminatory in his prank pulling—everyone got it.

Now, looking back on it from eighty years in the future, I realize that I owe Talmage a debt of gratitude. He was a good teacher; from him I learned not only the art of pulling pranks but one particular lesson that would stick with me for life.

This one prank was well thought out, perhaps verging on genius. One fine day, Talmage and I were out in a field behind the house doing chores. Once we were done feeding the calves, he took a chocolate candy bar out of his shirt pocket with more than the usual flair, accounted for my having noticed it, and took a bite, then put it back in his pocket. He paused. "Herbie," he said sweetly, "would you like a bite?" Now, Talmage was not the kind of uncle who'd share his chocolate with a pesky little nephew out of the goodness of his heart. Red flag. Big red flag. HUGE red flag. I didn't see it.

"Yes!" I practically shouted.

Talmage reached into his shirt pocket, took out a bar, holding it so his hand covered most of it and only an edge was available to bite. He held it out for me. I took as big a bite as I could.

Instead of my mouth filling with the heavenly taste of chocolate, it filled with the taste of . . . my mom's cleaning vinegar. No, mouse droppings. Dirt mixed with twigs. It was disgusting. I didn't want Talmage to get mad at me, so I did the opposite of what I wanted to do, which was spit it out. That's right: I swallowed it.

"Did you just swallow that?" Talmage asked.

"Yes," I said, my stomach beginning to churn.

"That's chewing tobacco, you dim-witted dodo! You should've spit it out. It'll make you sick."

His prediction soon came to pass. Saliva poured into my mouth as my stomach cramped and the world spun, round and round and round and round. Suddenly, I was throwing up, on my hands and knees on the ground. *I'm dying,* I thought, almost hopeful about it. I would welcome anything that would stop the pain.

That was the first and probably the only time Talmage ever felt bad about pulling one of his pranks on me. "It's OK, Herbie," he said once my stomach was emptied and then some. "You know, I wouldn't have given you that tobacco if I thought you were going to swallow it. Let's get you over to the hose so we can wash your mouth out." Because of his genuine concern, I did not tell on him. Anyway, I was embarrassed for having been fooled yet again.

Though the experience was horrible at the time, it turned out that Talmage had done me a big favor. Most every kid will try tobacco in some form at least once in their lifetime, and that was my own personal experiment, one that I will never forget. It was the one and only time that any tobacco product touched or passed my lips, all because of my uncle's underhanded prank.

Talmage, a belated thank-you.

FREE SWIMMING LESSONS

It was one of those typical September days in Arizona, hot and sunny with the temperature over 100 degrees Fahrenheit. All of us kids except Callis were at my aunts and uncles' place, where a large irrigation ditch ran behind the house. The ditch was about eight feet wide, the water four feet deep with a steady flow, and spanned by a bridge with a headgate at the edge of their property.

The big kids liked to play in it for fun and to cool off on hot days such as this one. They were playing in it now, splashing around, jumping off the headgate bridge, dunking one another, doing the things that big kids like to do. How I wished I was in that water too, splashing and dunking and, most of all, cooling off. But to me it was forbidden. My parents claimed that the water was too deep for a five-year-old. Oh, and there was the minor detail of my not being able to swim.

So there I was, running up and down the bank, over and back across the bridge, building up a sweat and watching my aunts and uncles and cousins and their friends having what looked like the best time ever. Suddenly, Talmage and Junior grabbed me from behind.

"Hey!" I shouted. "Lemme go!" Of course, they ignored my cries and, instead, picked me up and carried me over to the headgate bridge. Once we were standing on it over the ditch, Talmage took my ankles and Junior took my wrists. In unison, as though they had been planning it, they said, "Time for you to learn how to swim!" Then they started swinging me. "One . . ." Out I swung, then back, then out again. "Two . . ."

"No no no no no!" I screamed. "I can't swim!"

"Three!" they said and let me go. I sailed out over the ditch. "Swim, Herbie, swim!" were the last words I heard before I hit the water.

There was a big splash, and then silence. I opened my eyes. The sun was shining down, the distorted rays of light beaming through the water. For a moment, I looked around. My aunts and cousins were there, minus their heads, which were up above the surface.

My feet hit the bottom, and instinct took over. I pushed with all my might, then came up gasping for air, flailing my arms about and kicking my legs spasmodically, somehow managing to stay afloat. The water flowed downstream, pulling me along with it. Gradually, as my initial panic subsided, I stopped flailing and began an impromptu dog paddle, desperately trying to keep my head above the water. *I can swim!* I thought. *Look, everyone, I can swim! I'm doing it, I'm swimming!*

Three of the girls were paddling beside me, yelling encouragement. "You're swimming, you're swimming, keep going, you can do it!" They steered me—and by "steered" I mean pushed—me away from the edge and back toward the middle of the ditch as I tried to get to land. Later I realized that they had been trying to help me reach the cottonwood tree root that stuck out of the bank and made a perfect step for the bigger kids.

Unfortunately, for a little guy like me, one who only *thought* he could swim, it was something of a challenge getting out of the ditch. "Hold on here, Herbie," Falene said, grabbing my hand and placing it on the root. "Now put your foot here. OK, good, now pull yourself up." With a lot of help, I managed to get out of the water and, crawling on my hands and knees, up onto the bank. Before I could catch my breath, Talmage and Junior came running, yelling, "It's time for lesson number two!"

I stood up and took off, zigzagging along the bank of the ditch, looking back now and then to check the progress of my pursuers. I was more concerned about getting away from them than I was with watching where I was going. Talmage and Junior didn't even have to toss me off the bridge this time to give me another swimming lesson—I took a false step, tripped, and found myself back in the water. The girls came to my rescue yet again, swimming alongside me and yelling, "You can do it, you can do it, keep swimming!" as I made my way back to the tree root. Talmage and Junior laughed and laughed.

I did a better job the second time around. Arvilla helped me out of the water and back up onto the bank, where I immediately scoped the terrain for Talmage and Junior. In the water? No. On my side of the bank? Gloriously not. On the other side? Nope. On the bridge? Uh-uh. They were nowhere in sight.

I sat down and leaned back, letting the sun dry my skin, and took a deep breath. *Aaah,* I thought, my muscles good and tired. I started to feel sleepy, my eyelids heavy . . . and there they were, jumping out from behind the giant cottonwood tree. "Lesson number three!" they yelled, grabbing me under the arms and lifting me off the ground. They carried me at a run all the way back to the headgate bridge. With a "One . . . two . . . three" they launched me into the air toward lesson number three.

By this time, I'd gotten the hang of it and, after the initial shock of hitting the water, was really swimming, actually dog-paddling, keeping my head above the water all the way to the tree root, where the girls were waiting. Maxine, Falene, and Arvilla, relieved that the boys had taken a break from splashing and dunking them in order to "teach" me to swim, were enjoying helping me out. They got to practice their nurturing skills, Talmage and Junior got the joy of making my life miserable, and I got to learn to swim. It was a win-win-win situation for all of us.

Soon enough, the boys tired of their little game, and the girls had had enough of babysitting, and that was that. I don't recommend this kind of swimming lesson, but in the end it worked—I now knew how to swim.

A DAY OF SPEECHES

When I wasn't getting up to trouble at my uncles' and cousins' high school, I was seeking after-school adventures on the campus of Arizona State Teachers College, now known as Arizona State University. One midwinter afternoon, I saw a small group of students gathered at the west end of Old Main, a stately three-story building built in 1898. I went over to check it out.

I quickly realized that, at my height, getting close to the crowd wasn't the best idea in terms of being able to see what was going on. I climbed partway up a nearby set of stairs to get a better view. Standing on a wooden box was a tall, thin man, a little older than most of the crowd of students, speaking enthusiastically and gesturing with his hands. When he finished, the students cheered and threw coins at his feet, on the ground around the wooden box.

I couldn't for the life of me imagine why they were throwing their money away. If they didn't want it, I'd take it! I made my way to the middle of the group and got down on my hands and knees, stuffing my pockets with as many coins as I could get. The speaker was involved in a discussion with some of the remaining students and wasn't paying attention, and no one else tried to stop me. Looking back, I think they must have thought I was the speaker's son.

By the time the school bell started ringing, my pockets were sagging with the weight of coins. I hurried through the crowd and ran back across the street, taking up my pose of innocence on the swing and awaiting Maxine and Falene's arrival.

On the way home, I just couldn't keep the story of my newfound fortune to myself.

"I saw all these people cheering and throwing their money away!" I told my aunts. I didn't mention the fact that I happened to be on the college campus at the time. "Look, I filled up my pockets!"

Of course, they didn't believe my story.

"You're lying," said Falene.

"Yeah, you probably stole all that money," added Maxine.

"Did not!" I said.

Before we'd even crossed the front-door threshold, Maxine was yelling to Grandma.

"Mama, Mama! Herbie is a liar and a thief!" My mom and grandma were in the kitchen, preparing a snack for us.

"What's this all about?" my grandmother wanted to know. "Herbie?"

Now, you didn't lie to Mom and Grandma, especially Grandma. After raising nine kids, she could read body language like a book; she knew you were getting ready to tell a lie before you even opened your mouth. So I confessed everything.

Mom yielded to Grandma, thinking her mother could probably handle this one better than she could. Grandma got an empty fruit jar out of the cupboard. "All right, Herbie, empty your pockets." I did as I was told, putting all those beautiful coins into the jar. I felt my cheeks turning red, a mixture of embarrassment and disappointment. She wouldn't even let me count the money. "That's not yours, and, anyway, we're going to return it to its rightful owner."

As we walked to the college, Grandma held my hand and helped me prepare my "I'm sorry" speech. Once on campus, we headed toward Old Main, Grandma asking passersby if they knew where the speaker who'd just been there had gone. Finally, she found someone who looked at me and said she'd heard a story about a little boy taking some money and running away. She promised she'd find the graduate student who'd given the speech and see to it that he got his money back.

"Do you have something you'd like to say?" my grandmother asked, nudging me forward.

"I'm sorry," I said. My grandmother handed me the jar, which I handed to the speaker's friend. "I thought people were throwing money away and they didn't want it, so I took it. I didn't know I was stealing it. I won't never do it again."

On the way home, I got a well-deserved lecture about why the money was tossed to the man.

"It was to say thank you for his speech," Grandma said.

I still didn't understand. "But why didn't the students just hand it to him instead of throwing it at him? It looked like they were throwing it away."

"That's just how it's done when someone gives a speech."

I thought, but didn't say, that I wished someone had thrown coins at me after my "I'm sorry" speech.

HOME SWEET HOME

Finally, our new adobe home was ready. Dad had spent the whole day on the finishing touches, painting the last window frame just as the sun set. The paint would be dry by morning, and we would have a place of our own, hopefully without scorpions. Mom and Dad were excited, while I had mixed feelings because I would miss living with Grandma, Grandpa, Maxine, Falene, Callis, and Talmage. Well, not so much Talmage.

Like my grandparents and the lumberjacks at the house in the woods, my dad knew that putting me to work was the best way to keep me out from underfoot. It was also a good way to build my self-esteem (not that the term "self-esteem" was in common usage then). He had me do many important jobs, like holding the end of the tape measure while he measured something, picking up scraps of wood and putting them in the kindling pile, sweeping up sawdust, holding the board steady while he sawed off the other end, throwing straw into the adobe mud. I'd even helped him carry lumber, when it wasn't too big. I was proud of our accomplishment and felt that it was my house, too.

We didn't have much to move. What little furniture we had—a couple of upholstered chairs, a floor lamp, Mom and Dad's bed, my little bed, Patsy's crib, a chest of drawers, a small kitchen table with four chairs, my high chair, Mom's vanity, and the boxes packed with the rest of our stuff— we loaded onto the back of Grandpa's flatbed truck. Mom wrapped the mirror of her vanity in a blanket, then made sure that the men took special care with it so that it wouldn't get scratched. The clothes and bedding went in the rumble seat of the Model A.

Grandpa drove the truck, Grandma sitting beside him. It was Saturday, so Callis and Talmage were free to help. They rode in the back of the truck with the furniture. How I envied them. I was a big boy—I could help build a house, I could swim, and I was six years old now—and thought I was big enough to ride in the back of the truck, too. Alas, I had to ride in the Model A with Mom and Dad.

The rumble seat was full of boxes, so I rode in my next-favorite spot, standing on the floorboard in front of Mom. Remember, this was long before child seats or seat belts were invented. From this vantage point I could see out the windshield and Mom's window. Outside, farmers drove tractors, and cows grazed in the yellow-green fields.

When we got to the farm, Dad pulled one of his great diversion maneuvers, sending me over to unwrap bread and put it in the swill barrels. It was a chore that I liked doing, in large part because I'd sneak a bite of cupcake or donut before tossing it. If I was really lucky, I would get there before the other farmhands took the best of the pickings, and I'd grab a box or two of donuts and run them over to the house for Dad. He liked to start the day with a hot cup of the coffee substitute Postum, with cream and a couple of donuts to hold him over until Mom cooked breakfast. I guess the only reason I wasn't as fat as the pigs was that I was always moving. How my grandmother and mother wished I would just sit still every once in a while!

It's interesting how a person's perspective colors their attitude. Mom thought that our little three-room adobe house with a bath and a corrugated galvanized metal roof was the "cat's meow," as she would say. At that time in her life, when she only had my grandparents' farm, a trailer in the woods, and a house full of scorpions to compare it to, it probably was. A decade or two later, she would have thought it was a sad little mud shack and felt sorry for the people who had to live in it.

I don't remember if it had an inside toilet or an outhouse, but it did have running water for the kitchen and bathing. On the inside, the eight-inch-thick earthen walls were finished with a smooth surface and painted white. The living area, where the two upholstered chairs, Patsy's high chair, and the kitchen table and chairs were stationed, was rather dim in the evenings. Besides the floor lamp, the only light came from a single light bulb hanging from the ceiling over the table.

I do remember Dad going out of his way to make our home cozier. As the romantic type, he would bring Mom flowers, either wildflowers that grew in the field or around the house. She would put them in a mason jar filled with water, then wrap a ribbon around the neck to hide the lid threads and tie it in a bow. If there was any raised writing on the jar, she would turn it to face away so that it couldn't be seen. She was as proud of her mason jar of flowers as if it were a crystal vase.

Sometimes, after dinner, Dad would lean over and whisper in my ear, "Go get the flashlight and try to find your mom a cake. I think I saw a few coconut cakes come in earlier today." That was her favorite.

My mission was to find a coconut cake that was still in the box, in one piece, and not smashed, which was quite a feat. Can you imagine being six years old, facing a mountain of bread and boxes of baked goods three times your height in the dark? I remember the sound of crickets chirping, the smell of vanilla and yeast and hay and pigs all around as the stars twinkled above.

It was fun climbing around in the pile, the moon providing enough light to make out shapes. When I saw a box that looked square and intact, I'd shine my flashlight on it, and I got pretty good at locating cakes, cupcakes, pies, jelly rolls, and donuts. Usually I'd keep looking until I found two desserts that were in good shape—one for Mom, one for Dad and me.

ALL GOOD THINGS MUST COME TO AN END

The price of pork had risen fast in the spring of 1939, and so a lot of farmers had invested in pigs, including Bishop Turley. Because of this, in early 1940, the market had been flooded, and the price of pork started dropping. The government stepped in to control this by buying piglets and sows, and Turley jumped at the chance to get out of the market.

Shortly after the last of the pigs had been trucked out in double-decker semitrailers, we packed up our belongings and left. We'd lived in the adobe house for only six or seven months. With the number of mines in the Globe and Miami area, jobs were always available. Dad quickly found work in a copper mine in Globe. That's where I finished first grade.

CHAPTER 5

The Corner of Alma School Road and Apache Trail: 1940–1942

Cliffs ran along one side of the winding road between Globe and Superior; on the other side mountains rose up into the sky. I had the best seat on the Greyhound bus, the first seat on the passenger side, and an unobstructed view through the large windshield. I was excited; Dad was working in a mine outside of Globe, and I was on my way to live with Grandpa and Grandma again, this time on their farm in Mesa, and start second grade at Alma Elementary School.

Mom had packed a small suitcase with my clothes and a cardboard box with my other stuff and written a note with my name, where I was to get off the bus, and the names of Grandpa and Grandma on it and pinned it on my shirt with a safety pin so that I wouldn't lose it. At the Greyhound bus station, she had talked at length with the bus driver, while I looked around at all the people coming and going. "Let me see that note," he'd said, gently lifting it away from my shirt so he could read it. "The bus goes right by that corner of Alma School Road and Apache Trail, ma'am, and I'll make sure your boy gets off the bus there." It was 1940, and sending off an unaccompanied minor with a note pinned to his shirt was no big deal.

The driver took my suitcase and cardboard box and loaded them in the luggage compartment. After I said goodbye and succumbed to an embarrassing goodbye kiss from Mom, the driver took me by the hand and escorted me to the door of the bus. There was a couple sitting in the first seat; the driver asked them to move since he needed to keep an eye on me.

Mesa is about seventy-five miles from Globe. In 1940, there were no freeways, and Highway 60 was just a two-lane road, the first half winding through mountains and hills. The trip was about three hours long, with three stops in Miami, Superior, and Mesa. I hadn't yet learned to read a clock, not that there were any on the bus, and I had no idea how long it would take. Though I'd initially been excited, after a while of watching the road, thinking we would be there any minute yet still not arriving, I got bored and tired, so I lay down on the seat and fell asleep.

The next thing I heard was "Herbie, wake up, it's time to get off the bus." We were at the corner of Alma School Road and Apache Trail, a wagon trail-turned-road that leads to Roosevelt Dam and Tonto National Monument. As promised, the driver had made this extra stop to drop me off. I stood up and followed him down the stairs, hopping off the last one to the ground. I looked around; my grandparents weren't there.

"Sorry, son," the driver said, retrieving my suitcase and box and setting them as far off the edge of the road as he could. "I can't wait here with you. I got a schedule to keep and a bunch of passengers who've got somewhere to be. You go ahead and sit on your suitcase, I'm sure your grandparents will be here any minute."

I did as he suggested, watching the back of the bus as it drove away. Around me were the open fields and sun-worn fences and great blue sky of home. I was happy to be in familiar terrain but a little bit worried. What if Grandma and Grandpa forgot? Were they ever going to get here? In reality, I probably spent less than five minutes sitting on the side of the road, all alone, before they arrived. The sight of them approaching filled me with relief. (As it was, the distance between the corner and their driveway was only about the length of a football field; I'm sure I could've figured it out if push came to shove.)

Grandma hugged me and kissed me, and Grandpa ruffled my hair, then picked up my box. Grandma carried my suitcase in one hand and held my hand with the other. As soon as we got to the farm, she said, "Let's do the old 'cheat Ma Bell' trick." Ma Bell was what folks called the Bell System, the original telephone monopoly named for the inventor Alexander Graham Bell. In those days, you could not call long distance directly; you had to call the operator, and she would make the call for you, then connect you when the person on the other end answered. If you just gave her the phone number, she would automatically connect you, and you would be charged for the call. If you told the operator you were calling person-to-person and gave a name, when someone answered the phone, the operator would say she had a person-to-person call for that individual. If they were there and answered the phone, a higher long-distance charge would start. If the person was not there, then there would be no charges.

In 1940, long-distance phone calls were approximately four cents per mile, so making a phone call from my grandparents' farm to Globe cost about three dollars—about one day's income for a farmer. To cheat Ma Bell, Grandma would tell the operator that she wanted to make a person-to-person long distance call to Herb Bryce. The operator would find the number for my parents, call them, and say she had a person-to-person call for Herb Bryce. Mom would say I wasn't there, which was true. This was Grandma's way of letting Mom know I had made the trip safe and sound without paying for a long-distance call.

THE SCHOOL OF HARD KNOCKS

After Grandma fed me and wiped off my fresh milk mustache, Grandpa asked me if I wanted to come along to check on the irrigation. This was to be the start of a bond that grew stronger as the years went by, the beginning of a transition from Grandma's boy to Grandpa's boy. My uncles—Talmage, who was now twenty years old, and Callis, now nineteen—had moved to Los Angeles to work in the defense industries, leaving me as Grandpa's only male family member helper. At least, I thought I was his helper. Whenever he left the house I was like a little puppy, right there beside him, tagging along everywhere he went. He would even let me sit in his lap in the tractor, his hands over my hands on the steering wheel, giving me the impression that I was steering.

Grandpa was very good at explaining what he was doing and why. At first, to my six-year-old ears, it was all mumbo jumbo, but as time went by, his explanations started to make sense. When I think about those early years with Grandpa, I wonder: Did his explaining the what, where, and why of everything develop my scientific thinking, or was I born with a scientific style of thinking that allowed me to understand what Grandpa was saying? That's one of those unanswerable chicken-or-egg questions. Either way, what a great teacher Grandpa was, patient and gentle and generous.

After checking on the irrigation, Grandpa said, "Now that the boys are gone, you're going to have to learn about the farm. If you're going to live with us, I expect you to pay for your keep." He spelled out in detail what this would look like. "You'll gather the eggs every day for your breakfast. You'll feed the poultry—that'll earn you your lunch. For your dinner, fill the rabbits' water bowls and cut alfalfa to feed them. When I'm splitting the wood for the stove, I'll cut up some kindling, and you'll need to take it in and put in Grandma's kindling box—that's for a bed to sleep in. Think you can do all that?"

Feeling like a big boy, I answered, "I can do that."

"You promise?"

"I promise."

"I will help you for a few days so you can learn how to do it."

Nowadays, perhaps that would be called child indentured servitude. But for me it was a great life-changing lesson. I had to earn my keep, and I felt like my work was valuable to the farm and the family. Grandpa always did know how to make me feel important.

An even bigger lesson came about three weeks later. One day, I forgot to collect the eggs, and so, the next morning, I came into the main part of the house to find that my place at the table had not been set, and my chair was pushed back against the wall. I started dragging my chair to the table, and Grandpa said, "You don't get breakfast this morning 'cause you didn't gather the eggs yesterday like you promised you would. No eggs, no breakfast."

"I'll go get them now."

"It's too late, Herbie. Grandma had to gather them this morning for our breakfast."

I couldn't believe it. The unfairness of it all! Grandpa assured me, "There will be more eggs this afternoon for you to gather to pay for tomorrow's breakfast. Now go sit in your chair while we say the blessing. After, you can sit in your chair while we eat, or you can go outside and play until we are through."

I climbed up on the chair, trying my best not to pout. My stomach rumbled. How would I survive until lunch? Grandpa asked my aunt Maxine to say the blessing. I think she felt sorry for me because, at the end, she added, ". . . and bless Herbie so that he won't get too hungry, and help him to keep his promises. Amen."

As soon as I heard the "amen," I got up and went outside, not to play but to hide so that no one would see me cry. I kicked up some dirt, sniffling and wiping my eyes, and threw a few rocks at the chicken house. "Stupid chickens," I mumbled. But I knew it was entirely my fault. Images of buttered biscuits, eggs with lacy golden edges hot from the frying pan, and glasses of fresh milk filled my mind, and my stomach rumbled again. If only I had gathered the eggs yesterday as promised, I would be eating right now. Not only was I hungry, I was upset for letting Grandpa down. I vowed that I would never forget my chores again. To guarantee my lunch, I scattered some feed on the ground for the ducks and chickens. When I went to get the water for their water bowls, I saw through the kitchen window my aunts Falene and Maxine washing the dishes.

Grandma was standing at the door with the chipped ceramic pie pan full of breakfast scraps in her hand. "Will you feed the chickens?" she said, handing it to me. I nodded, then started to turn around. Grandma stopped me. "Hold on, Herbie, I forgot to put these in the scrap pan." She held out two biscuits. "I got them ready with butter and honey, but then I was too full to eat them. I'm sure the chickens won't mind." She carefully placed them on top of the other scraps. I headed out to the chicken coop, keeping one hand on the biscuits so they wouldn't fall off. Those two biscuits the chickens never saw. Boy, did they ever taste good.

Several years later, Grandpa admitted that they'd planned the whole thing after they'd discovered that I hadn't brought in the eggs. "Grandma came up with the biscuit and honey idea and having Maxine include 'bless Herbie so he won't get too hungry' in the blessing," he told me. "I added 'and to help him to keep his promises.' Falene didn't think one biscuit would be enough, so we decided to make it two biscuits." We both laughed over that, and how I'd fallen for it. It is a lesson that remained with me all my life: there ain't no such thing as a free breakfast.

A WISH COME TRUE

Grandpa placed his two little fingers in the corners of his mouth and let out the familiar loud, shrill milking whistle. Then he yelled "Suuzzzyy-Q!" Suzy-Q lifted her head, looked toward us, and headed our way at a trot. Right on cue the rest of the cows started crowding together; they knew it was milking time. I was so excited for Suzy-Q to get to me that, unable to wait, I ran as fast as I could toward her. We met halfway, and I jumped on her back, rode her out to round up the other cows, and herded them into the corral. Grandpa closed the gate behind us.

This was my favorite chore on the farm. It sure beat feeding the calves and slopping the pigs. But I had even bigger dreams. Today was my seventh birthday, and, by gum, my birthday wish was going to come true.

Earlier that day, Maxine had come looking for me. She found me playing with the milk separator, a centrifugal device that separates raw milk into cream and skim milk. The separator had a bell incorporated into the handle, and I was trying to figure why, if you turned it slow, the bell would ring twice with each rotation, once when it was at the top and again when it was at the bottom. The bell stopped ringing, however, when you turned it fast. Grandpa had told me that the bell's ringing was a warning to let you know that you were turning the handle too slow. When you started turning the handle, the bell would ring until you reached the right speed for maximizing the separation of the cream from the milk. I was interested in physics even at that age.

Milk separator, 1930s. This machine separates the cream from the milk.

"Grandma wants to see you," Maxine had said. I let go of the separator handle and followed her out of the barn. Inside the house, Grandpa, Falene, and Grandma were holding a birthday cake with seven candles. They started singing "Happy Birthday." I already knew what my wish was; I had been thinking about it for a while. When they got to the final line of the song, I closed my eyes, silently said my wish to myself, and blew hard. When I opened my eyes, there were seven flameless, smoking candles, meaning my wish was going to come true.

"What'd you wish for?" Grandma asked.

"Yeah, whaddju wish for, Herbie?" said Falene.

"Don't tell," said Maxine. "If you do, it won't come true."

"But I need to tell Grandpa, or it *can't* come true," I replied. She thought a minute, then said, "Well, I guess that'll be OK. But only tell him!"

Grandpa leaned down so I could whisper in his ear, "I want to milk seven cows tonight." He raised an eyebrow, giving me that "you gotta be kidding" look, and said, "Wow! Did I hear you right? You want to do what?"

I leaned in closer and whispered again, "I want to milk seven cows tonight."

"That sure is a strange birthday wish, but if that's what you want, I'll see to it that it comes true." He turned to Grandma and remarked, "Herbie and I are going out to the shed to make sure the kerosene lamps are full. We are going to need them tonight."

Grandpa and I set off together. Out of earshot of Grandma and the girls, he asked, "Herbie, what's gotten into your head? I must have been at least twelve or thirteen before I milked seven cows. What makes you think you can milk seven cows at your age?"

"Grandpa, I milked four cows last night. I know I can milk seven tonight."

"You know that I'll have to milk my twelve cows *and* strip your seven, like I did those four you milked last night, don't you?" Stripping involves getting the very last bit of milk from the udder in order to prevent mastitis, an inflammation of the mammary gland, typically due to bacterial infection. Stripping prevents a path for the bacteria. Present-day dairies use a dip or spray to disinfect the teats, but back then we used a couple of tablespoons of bleach in water and a special grip with the thumb, forefinger, and palm to make sure all the milk had been squeezed out, a grip that is difficult for young or inexperienced milkers. "It'll be really tough, Herbie."

"Please, please, let me try."

"OK, but if your arm muscles cramp up, you'll have to stop and let me finish. Promise?"

"I promise." I was determined to be a real farm boy, not just a boy on a farm.

We didn't have a designated milking barn; in fact, we didn't have buildings of any kind out where we milked the cows, nor stalls or a slab of concrete for the cows to stand on, or stanchions, devices with two vertical bars, one stationary and one that can pivot at the base to be opened for the cow to stick her head in and then shut around her neck so that she stays still, happily munching grain while you milk her. All we had was a small fenced-off corral in one corner of a large alfalfa field, which would accommodate thirty or forty cows and was close to the road so that we wouldn't have to carry the full ten-gallon milk cans very far to be picked up by the creamery's flatbed truck every morning and evening. A couple of cottonwood trees growing on the bank of the irrigation ditch provided some shade. The ground had no vegetation except for some hay that had already been digested and deposited there in the form of "cow pies," which dry quickly in the arid climate of Arizona. Once or twice a week, we would get the tractor out to scrape the dry manure into a mound to be used at a later date for fertilizing the crops.

Milking by hand, let alone milking outside in a corral covered in dry manure, made our milk officially unfit to be bottled and sold in stores. Because of that, we sold it to a Borden factory to be canned. Producing canned milk required evaporation to remove 60 percent of the water, followed by its being homogenized, canned, and sterilized in a canning retort (a huge commercial pressure cooker), heated to 240 to 245 degrees Fahrenheit. The process is more than enough to kill off any and all bacteria that might have made it through the filter.

Grandpa had a few hours before milking time in which to mull over his cow selection. Some cows are more difficult to milk; some are easier. The more a heifer wants to keep her milk, the tighter you have to squeeze to take it away from her. For a seven-year-old boy determined to set a new personal record, you want a docile cow that "gives up" her milk easily. You don't want to have to use hobbles, a device used to prevent kicking that consists of two metal pieces shaped to fit the hind legs above the hocks and connected in front by a chain. You want the cow's teats to be at least as long as the width of your palm, if not longer, so you can use all of your fingers to force the milk out. If they're shorter than the width of your hand, you will have to milk with fewer fingers to extract the same amount of milk.

For example, Suzy-Q was great to ride but hell to milk. She had stubby teats. If cows wore bras, hers would be a double A. They were so short that, as a teenager, I could only milk her with two fingers. Believe me, a thumb and four fingers work a lot better than a thumb and two fingers. Add to that the problem of trying to keep the other two fingers and lower part of your palm out of the way so the milk won't run down your hand on its way to the bucket.

By the time the cows were ready for their evening milking, Grandpa had picked out seven of the most docile of the bunch, including one named Milton. That's right: Milton. My uncle Milton had given my grandparents a cow to take care of while he was off prospecting in the mountains. He hadn't named her, and so we initially referred to her as Milton's cow. After a while we dropped the possessive and started calling her, simply, "Milton." If I had a heifer—not a bull—named after me, I would've been embarrassed, but I don't think Uncle Milton seemed to mind. Or maybe he didn't know.

I strapped on my one-legged milking stool, grabbed my milk bucket, and headed over to Heidi, my favorite. All of our cows had names, not numbers—it was a small enough herd that we could tell them apart, saving them from having to get a tag clipped onto their ears like cows do on large commercial farms.

"Hold on there, Herbie," Grandpa said before I began. "You see how Milton's teats are dripping milk? Start with her."

I moved over and set to washing Milton's udder and teats. I settled down on my stool and placed the bucket on the ground between my feet. I didn't yet have the leg strength to hold a whole bucket of milk between my knees like Grandpa did.

And so my birthday wish began to come true. I placed my thumb on the udder just above the teat, wrapped my fingers firmly around it, then exerted a slight pressure downward with the thumb, squeezing with the top finger and then progressively squeezing down the line, from the second finger to the third finger to the little finger. This takes significant dexterity; often new milkers will inadvertently start with the little finger and work up toward their thumb, which ends up pushing the milk toward the udder and making the cow extra grumpy.

I knew I was doing it right when the milk squirted out. Once I had it going, I grabbed another teat with my other hand and start the squeezing procedure. From watching

Grandpa I knew that I wanted to get a rhythm going, alternating between the right hand and the left, applying more pressure with every squeeze and picking up the tempo. Pretty soon the squirts became streams. Grandpa could usually get it so that the milk was streaming with such force that it produced foam on top of the milk in the bucket. (He also had such control that he could knock a fly off the rim of the bucket with a well-aimed squirt.) When you can get a thick layer of foam, you have arrived.

Now, stop and think. Every cow has four teats, each of which needs to be milked. That's a lot of work. Consider, too, how many squirts are required for every gallon of milk. I can tell you, it's a lot, particularly back then; today's cows have been bred to produce at least twice as much as our cows did.

Me milking Heidi.

When I finished milking Milton—*I* was finished, even if the job wasn't—I carried my bucket over to the ten-gallon milk can and poured the milk through the strainer into the can. Now on to number two, a calm little Jersey named Heidi. I let Grandpa know that Milton was ready to be stripped. "OK," he said. "I'll strip her to make sure the udder is empty when I'm through here."

After Heidi, it was on to number three, Bessie, then Beulah, then Gertie. By now the sun had set, so Grandma lit the four kerosene lanterns hanging on the fence. I had to herd my last two cows over to the light so that I could see what I was doing. Grandpa and Grandma had finished milking their cows and were sitting next to each other on their stools and talking when the milk truck pulled up. The driver unloaded our empty milk cans with a series of clangs, then started loading the recently filled milk cans onto the truck. Grandpa came over to where I was sitting with cow number six, took my bucket, and emptied what was in it into the strainer. With a rising panic I watched him return the bucket to me and then remove the strainer from the last milk can. I knew I was in trouble; I hadn't gotten my seven cows milked in time, even though we'd started a half hour earlier than normal. What was I going to do?

Grandma noticed my distress and came over to try to calm me down. "It's all right," she said. "Your grandpa and I talked it over, and we decided that I'll use any milk that doesn't make it onto the creamery truck to make butter, buttermilk, and cottage cheese. You know how Grandpa loves his fresh buttermilk." That made me feel a little bit better. Imagining fresh biscuits slathered with butter made from cream from milk I'd gotten made me feel better, too.

"OK, Grandma," I said.

"How are your arms and hands doing?"

I attempted a smile. In all honesty, my muscles hurt so bad that I wanted to cry. But I was a big boy, and I'd been told, as many children of that era had, that big boys don't cry. All I had to do was finish milking this cow and then milk one more, and my birthday wish would come true. Then I could quit and go cry by myself. "They're not cramping up," I said, not technically lying, because though they were hurting like hell the cramping hadn't begun yet—it would arrive in full force later that night. I could see that Grandma didn't believe me. "I can finish," I assured her.

I'm sure that Grandpa did a lot more than just stripping of those last two cows.

Finally, long after the sun had gone to bed and the moon and stars had begun their night shift, I gave cow number seven a gentle pat on her flank and stood up, trying not to groan. I'd done it! I'd milked seven cows on my seventh birthday, a wish come true.

That night, Grandma and Grandpa were generous with their praise. "He milked all seven cows," Grandma told my aunts. I would guess that, in truth, I milked the first five cows about two-thirds of the way, and probably halfway for the last two. The evidence was in the weight of the bucket: a full milking would have weighed thirty to forty-five pounds, more than I could have lifted to the height needed to pour the milk into the strainer. My bucket, therefore, must have not been full. Grandpa did more than just stripping them; he finished milking them without a single word about it.

I could barely keep my eyes open long enough to eat supper. Shortly after I collapsed into bed, the reality of milking seven cows struck. I woke up crying, the muscles in my arms and hands seizing, my fingers clenched so tightly that I couldn't open them. My sobs must have been pretty loud because Grandma came running, a bottle of Watkins Pain Relieving Liniment in her hand. She knelt next to my bedside. "Your arms are hurting pretty bad, aren't they?" she asked.

Not bothering to hide my tears, I said, "Yes, they hurt bad, real bad. I can't open my fingers, see?" Grandma poured some of the liniment into her hand, rubbed her hands together to warm it up, then began applying it to my arms and hands. *I'll never be able to milk again,* I was thinking.

She must have rubbed and massaged me for over an hour, reassuring me the whole time that the pain would go away. It took her a long time to coax my fingers into unclenching.

"I'll talk to Grandpa about you going back to milking only two or three cows, then increasing the number one at a time until you're back up to seven. You have to work at making your muscles stronger a little at a time so they won't hurt like this again." I sniffled and nodded, not totally convinced that I'd ever be able to milk even one cow, let alone seven.

But her plan worked, and in about three weeks, I was back up to seven. Then Grandpa upped the ante. "Now that you are back to seven cows," he said, "it's time to start working on stripping your cows dry." Whenever I thought I had it down perfect, he'd come over and show me that I hadn't gotten all of the milk. I was a devoted student, and on every test, he got a little less milk. It took a few months, but I finally got there. By that time I realized that this was not just a way to prove myself—milking cows was hard, everyday work.

The whole time, Grandma and Grandpa were quick to tell anyone who would listen about my birthday accomplishment. Never once did I hear them downplay it by saying they had to strip or finish milking the cows. They gave me full credit.

As an adult looking back on my seventh birthday, I realize just how great Grandma's and Grandpa's love and caring were. Neither one had completed grammar school. Neither one could have explained the stages of child development or defined psychology or used such terms as *self-esteem*, *empowerment*, or *learning through scaffolding*. But they put these ideas into practice every day, with their children and their grandchildren. They could have dismissed my wish as childish, or tried to talk me out of it, or said later that they really did most of the milking. But they knew how important it was for me to believe in myself, to try the impossible, to build my confidence, and to start understanding who I was. There is no greater way to demonstrate love, caring, and respect for a child. Their belief in me shaped my character and provided an example of the best way to view and treat others.

HANG UP MY BUCKET AND HEAD TO CALIFORNIA

In mid-April, Grandma gave me a big hug and said, "Your mom and dad will be here in two days to get you. They are moving to California and taking you with them. We love you very much and are going to miss you. Grandpa won't have his little helper."

I remember having mixed feelings. I think, at that time, I felt closer to my grandparents than to my parents. Helping Grandpa made me feel important, like a big boy. Every day after school, I went into the house, dropped off my lunch box, got a big hug from Grandma, then ran out to find Grandpa and help him run the farm. After what we on the farm called "supper," the light evening meal after the day's work was done, Falene or Maxine read me a story or sat with me while I drew pictures before bed.

The schedule with my parents was different. My dad left for work right after breakfast, not to be seen again until suppertime. Mom paid more attention to Patsy because she was still a little baby, and, instead of being the one to get fussed over, I was expected to make a fuss over her. Given the choice, I think I would have rather stayed on the farm. Even at seven, however, I knew that Mom and Dad had the final word about where I lived. I wonder if any of the adults in my life considered that I had only a couple of months left to

finish the second grade, and that it might have been worth-
while for me to see the school year through before moving
away.

But my parents had made the choice to uproot the
family out of financial necessity. In the spring of 1941,
Arizona was still struggling in the aftermath of the Great
Depression. Jobs continued to be scarce and wages were low.
Southern California, on the other hand, was booming, and
Los Angeles was the boomtown of boomtowns; it was the
fastest-growing area in the United States.

I was blissfully unaware of the larger factors that influ-
enced my own upheaval. In 1941, Congress had passed the
Lend-Lease Act so the United States could send war equipment, mainly aircraft, to meet Great Britain's demand as
they fought Nazi Germany. This caused a huge spike of
production in the military aircraft industry. The number of
military airplanes being produced went from 3,611 in 1940
to 18,466 in 1941, more than a 500 percent increase in a single year. Southern California had seven manufacturers and
over fifty aircraft "feeder plants" that were desperately looking for workers. The salary difference between a job mining
copper and a job building military aircraft was big enough
to get Dad's attention all the way in Arizona. Utopia was
only four hundred miles away.

Mom's three brothers and a couple of her sisters' husbands had already gotten jobs building airplanes in the Los
Angeles area. From them, she and Dad had been receiving
lots of one-cent postcards encouraging them to come out
and share the riches of California. In April, they couldn't
resist the call any longer. Dad gave his notice to the mining
company, and they hitched their two-wheel trailer to the
car, loaded up all their belongings, and headed west. On the
way, they stopped at Grandpa and Grandma's farm to pick

me up. Dad, Mom with Patsy in her lap, and me in the back seat were on our way to the land of milk and honey.

A TUMBLE DOWN THE STAIRS

Mom's oldest brother, Homer, his wife, Gladys, and their daughter, Nancy, were living in East Los Angeles. Talmage and Callis had followed them to California and were boarding with them. My folks wanted to be nearby, so they rented a small one-bedroom apartment above a detached garage a few blocks from where they lived.

Homer was what today we might call an overprotective father. I remember one visit in which Nancy, the cousin who had dropped me headfirst and broke my front tooth years before, and I were playing on the top landing of the apartment building's outside stairs. In my memory, the flight of stairs was dangerously steep, going down, down, down to the lawn below. Nancy was sitting at the edge of the top step, and then all of a sudden she was rolling like a boulder, screaming as she went. The door to our apartment was open, so everyone inside could hear her screams through the screen door. Homer, who always assumed the guilt of anyone within ten feet of his little angel, ran out, grabbed me by the arm, and started shaking me.

"What did you do to her?" he yelled. Noticing that his precious daughter wasn't in the vicinity, he looked around and saw her at the bottom of the stairs, lying flat on her back in the grass. The next question out of his mouth was "Why did you push her down the stairs?"

I told him I didn't push her, but he wasn't listening to me. No doubt he was thinking that since princesses don't fall, she must have been pushed. I'm sure I was thinking,

Don't you think you should go down and make sure she is still alive? Apparently reading my mind, Homer released me and ran down the stairs, toward the sound of Nancy's crying. In the end, she had several bruises but no broken bones. I'll admit, in my darker moments, my thoughts turned to revenge, and I secretly hoped that she had broken her front tooth. No such luck.

WHAT WAS THAT BUMP?

Shortly after settling in, I was hanging out with three new friends across the street from our apartment. We were playing marbles, sitting on the planting strip, my seat right at the edge where the grass met the concrete of the driveway. I had just won the game, and one of the boys leaned forward and playfully pushed me. Just as I fell over backward, a car backed out of the driveway and over my chest.

"Stop, stop, stop!" my friends yelled. The other boy got up and started banging on the car's fender. The driver pulled forward, running over my chest again. This time he stopped and got out of the car to see what all the ruckus was about.

Remember, cars in those days weighed at least three-quarters of a ton *less* than they do today. That's why I'm still alive. Still, I'm sure the sight of me lying on my back with tire tracks across my chest was a bit of a shock. The driver picked me up and laid me down in the back seat while his wife ran over to get Mom. He drove us straight to the emergency room, my head in my Mom's lap.

The good news was that they could not find any serious problems like, for example, crushed lungs or internal bleeding. Even so, the doctors wanted to keep me in the hospital for observation for a couple of days. My ribs hurt, but that didn't stop me from indulging in the all-you-can-eat supply of pudding or allowing the nurses to coddle me. The bad news was that I had two broken ribs—and a hefty hospital bill was on its way. The next afternoon, I awoke from a nap to overhear Mom and Dad talking in the hallway outside my room.

"How are we going to pay for all this?" Mom asked. Dad had not yet found a job, and I knew from other overheard conversations that their savings were getting low.

"I don't know," said my dad.

Fortunately, the car owner was insured. The best news of all was that, on top of my medical bills being covered, Mom and Dad received a check for $500. The average weekly wage in 1941 was $33, meaning such a sum was the equivalent of almost four months' pay. I went with my parents to pick up the check, feeling like I was saving the day like Captain Marvel, albeit Captain Marvel with a couple of broken ribs.

The insurance company was in downtown Los Angeles, on the top floor of what we thought of as a skyscraper. The height limit for buildings in Los Angeles at that time was only thirteen stories! I was so impressed by the view, the sprawl of the growing city. I thought I must be standing in the tallest building in the world. I had no idea about the 102-story Empire State Building, all the way across the country in New York City. Eastern Arizona was the farthest east I had ever been.

ANOTHER MOVE, ANOTHER SCHOOL

The apartment felt very small for four people, even if Patsy was only two years old. At the end of the school year, Mom and Dad went shopping for a new place to live. They found a two-bedroom apartment a couple of miles away, which meant I would be going to a different school. That would be the fifth school I attended, and I was only starting third grade! See the pattern?

Like most students, I began the school year on my best behavior. After a couple of weeks had gone by, that started to get old, and I decided that it was time to find out what I could get away with. I'd start small by sneaking a comic book into class.

During reading time, I opened my assigned "reader" and inserted a Captain Marvel comic book. Unfortunately, I hadn't realized that the comic was bigger than the reader, and the teacher, whom I will call "Miss Hawkeye," noticed the comic book pages sticking out. She walked up to my desk and simply confiscated Captain Marvel without a word. When the bell rang for recess, Miss Hawkeye told me to stay at my desk until she got back from walking the rest of the class outside.

When she got back, she sat down at the desk next to mine and gave me a little lecture. "You were not doing your reading assignment as directed," she said sternly.

"But it was reading time, and I was reading!" I argued.

Miss Hawkeye's eyebrows went up. Obviously, she was not convinced by this argument. "All right, Herb," she said, standing up. "Follow me." She walked over to the side black-boards and handed me a piece of chalk. "You're going to write 'I will not read comic books in class' fifty times. That's *fifty* times, and you'd better believe I'm going to count them when I get back from supervising recess. Now get started."

I looked up at the chalk-smudged expanse of the blackboard. Fifty times! I could already imagine how my shoulder would ache, not to mention the mind-numbing boredom such a punishment would induce. Then I saw the musical-staff chalk holder in the chalk tray, the kind that holds five pieces of chalk at a time so the teacher can draw five lines. Miss Hawkeye used it to make lines for showing us how to write cursive.

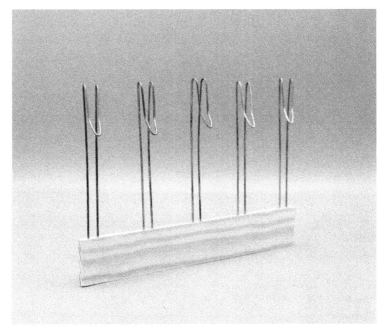

Musical-staff chalk holder.

I thought for a minute. The teacher had said that I had to write "I will not read comic books in class" fifty times. She did not say, "Write it one sentence at a time."

I picked up the chalk holder with its five pieces of chalk. It took me a few tries to get all five pieces of chalk to write at the same time and so the letters were small enough so as not to overlap. I was surprised to find that my experience with milking came in handy; I was dexterous and familiar with adjusting pressure. Once I got the hang of it, it didn't take very long. Instead of writing the sentence fifty times, I only had to write five sentences ten times. When the class came back in from recess, they found me sitting at my desk with a smirk on my face.

Seven-year-olds don't think like adults, especially like adult teachers. I was thinking, *Wow, I outsmarted the teacher. What a brilliant boy I am.* Meanwhile, the teacher knew there was something rotten in the state of Denmark. She walked over to my masterpiece and scanned the blackboard for a moment, then picked up the staff chalk holder. Maybe I hadn't outsmarted her after all. She turned toward me and, with a little chuckle, said, "We'll talk about this after school." She then went over to her desk and deposited the staff chalk holder in the bottom drawer.

I watched the clock tick. It's a fact that the more you dread something, the longer it takes to arrive. All day I worried about what would happen after school. Would she hit me with a ruler? Would she give me detention? Send me to the principal's office? Expel me from school forever?

Finally, the bell rang. To the rest of the class, the ringing was the sound of freedom. To me, it was the sound of impending doom.

Once all the kids had packed up their belongings and left the room, a few looking back over their shoulders to see how I was doing, the teacher slowly made her way to my desk, taking the same seat she had before.

"Well," she said nonchalantly, "what do you have to say for yourself?"

I'd come prepared. "You didn't say I had to write the sentences one at a time."

GRANDMA

Grandma was dying of cancer. I wasn't there when Mom got the news, and I wasn't privy to her and Dad's conversation about what they felt or discussions about what they were going to do. Back then, life, sickness, and death were more present yet not always openly discussed—people died of all kinds of illness we don't worry about today, and there were a million ways to get injured or killed on a farm, too. And, don't forget, we were in the throes of a world war, the second one of the century. Death was just part of life.

But this was *my* grandma. All I was told was that she was sick and that Mom and I were moving back to Mesa. I was in the middle of my third-grade school year, but that didn't matter. What mattered is that we were close to Grandma and Grandpa.

I don't remember much about the deterioration of Grandma's health, or even the details of her sickbed. I'm sure I was allowed to visit her bedside, at least when she wasn't asleep or in too much pain. What I do remember is Mom coming out of my grandparents' bedroom and saying, "The angels are standing at the foot of the bed." Grandma died that afternoon.

I didn't cry. That's just never been my way. I loved my grandma more than just about anyone, but I accepted that she was gone. And that was that.

Grandma's death left a big hole in Grandpa's life. The two of them had married as teenagers, welcomed eleven children into the world and said goodbye to two, worked together to feed their growing family. They were such good partners in life, and their marriage was loving, healthy, and strong. Grandpa would go on to have three more unions. But there was no replacing Grandma.

Mom decided that we would stay in Mesa. Someone needed to take over Grandma's work, and Falene was still in high school, Maxine in sixth grade. So we stayed, and I continued third grade at Alma School.

CORPORAL PUNISHMENT

I quickly settled back into school, walking or taking the bus the two or so miles every morning and afternoon. Many of the kids I knew from church, and I hadn't been gone all that long, so they remembered me. Soon enough I was getting up to my usual trouble.

One day, my friend Jackie and I were throwing dirt clods at each other. The thwack and crumble of a clod hitting someone is almost as satisfying as the sound of stomping mud. This day, Jackie happened to pick up a rock. He threw it and missed me but hit another student named Ramona in the forehead. She started crying when she saw blood dripping down her face.

We were sent to the principal's office. When he heard what had happened, he didn't waste any time taking us down to a room in the basement.

"Sit down," he said, pointing to a couple of chairs. I felt like a movie criminal about to be interrogated. First, he illuminated us with a little lecture on the danger of throwing rocks. I tried not to let my eyes glaze over. Then he said something that woke me up. "I've never had to paddle anybody, but I'm going to have to paddle you boys."

Back then corporal punishment was not just tolerated but endorsed in schools. He grabbed a board that had been leaning against the wall. It was eighteen inches long, with holes to eliminate drag, and a handle carved out of it. Instead of starting our beating, he sat down, took out a pocketknife, and continued to talk to us, all while whittling the holes. I'm sure he told the shop teacher to leave the paddle partially unfinished so he could do this performance. The rumor was that he would take it down and ask you to count the holes.

Jackie started crying. I remember thinking, *You can beat me, but I'm not going to cry.*

When the principal was done whittling, he asked me to count the holes. I did so without crying or fidgeting or letting fear creep into my voice. When I got to thirteen, the principal looked impressed. He told me to bend over and grab my ankles. I received my three swats without a sound.

This was not my only experience with "Spare the rod, spoil the child." One of my third-grade teachers had a stick she liked to pop kids with on the crown of the head if they did something wrong. It looked like a drumstick, with a ball on one end.

Apparently I hadn't learned my lesson after writing those fifty sentences at the school in Los Angeles, and I'd brought a comic book to class in Mesa. When the teacher saw me reading it, she didn't say a word before she knocked me on the back of the head. This made me mad.

"Ha ha," I said without thinking. "That didn't hurt."

And so she hit me harder, hard enough to hurt. I felt the back of my head and came away with a handful of blood. (To this day, I have a scar.) Terrified with the knowledge that she'd gone too far, the teacher grabbed a towel out of her desk drawer and pressed it to the wound. "I'm sorry," she whispered. Once the bleeding had stopped, she hid the bloody towel and broken stick at the bottom of the trash can, then escorted me to the nurse to get bandaged.

I didn't tell Mom or Grandpa. They would have sided with the teacher. I knew that if I got a swat at school, I'd get two at home. At least the teacher started being nice to me after that.

CHAPTER 6

Three Good Years in Goodyear: 1942–1944

President Roosevelt had been wary about involving the United States in the war in Europe since its beginning. He was happy, however, to have the US supply its allies with weapons, equipment, ships, and aircraft, knowing that the boom of this wartime production would serve to lift the country out of the Great Depression. The Lend-Lease Act, passed in March 1941, allowed the US to become involved in the war through these economy-boosting enterprises yet still maintain a distance.

The Goodyear Tire and Rubber Company had been making dirigibles for the Navy anti-submarine efforts in the Atlantic Ocean, the Pacific Ocean, and the Strait of Gibraltar, which prevented Germany's submarines from entering the Mediterranean Sea. In 1939, the company had branched out and created Goodyear Aircraft Company to build airframes, and soon the demand for aircraft sky-rocketed, maxing out Goodyear's Ohio-based factories.

Fortunately, Goodyear owned 36,000 acres of cotton fields west of Phoenix, Arizona, which they'd bought during World War I, when the Egyptian-grown cotton they'd been using in their tires had become unavailable. Now they could use some of that farmland to open an aircraft factory. The groundbreaking took place on July 15, 1941.

And not a second too soon. Not even five months later, on the morning of December 7, 1941, Japanese aircraft bombed Pearl Harbor. Within four days, we had declared war on both Japan and Germany. Building of aircraft was now critical—we needed to manufacture airplanes for our allies *and* for ourselves.

The pressure was on for the Goodyear Aircraft factory to be finished and fully operational. Of course, more work meant the need for more workers, and more workers meant the need for more housing. So Goodyear carved approximately one square mile out of their fifty-six square miles of cotton fields for their manufacturing plant, airfield, and living quarters for their workers. The Federal Housing Administration funded the building of 150 two-bedroom homes on forty acres of farmland kitty-corner from the factory. The Del Webb Construction Company was granted the contract, with the promise that they would get the job finished fast. If you owned a hammer and knew which end of the nail to hit, they'd hire you on the spot.

ANOTHER NEW HOME

This was a godsend for our family. Dad did indeed own a hammer and knew how to use it. Goodyear was less than forty miles from Mesa, and he was happy to get a construction job that would keep us in relative proximity to the family farm. Shortly after he hired on, Goodyear Aircraft advertised for welders, offering a salary that was more than he was making working for Del Webb. He had taught himself how to weld and was good at welding iron and steel but had never welded aluminum. When he inquired about the job, they offered to send him to Arizona State Teachers College to learn how to weld aluminum. That was the only class that Dad ever took at an institute of higher learning, but forever after Mom told people that her husband had graduated from Arizona State.

Mom and Dad bought one of the federally funded homes, and so we up and moved again. It was small, at approximately 750 square feet, and had two bedrooms, one bathroom, a combination living room and dining area, a very small kitchen, and a service porch. Dad turned the one-car garage into a wood and welding shop.

My aunt Falene moved in with us a few months later. She'd gotten married after my grandmother's (her mother's) death, the kind of rushed wedding that so many young people were having before the enlisted men had to leave for war. Her husband, Jearl, had gone overseas to serve in India. She was seventeen years old and eight months pregnant.

Falene's baby, Jearldene, was born just before three young men moved in. My uncle Talmage, my cousin Milton Jr., and their friend Joe Brown had also taken jobs at the Goodyear Aircraft factory and needed a place to live while they were waiting for their draft notices. Add my dad, my pregnant mom, my sister, and me, and the count was nine. That's nine people (including an infant and a toddler) crammed into 750 square feet. My sister Phyllis would be born soon thereafter, making it an even ten.

The kids' bedroom initially had two bunk beds and Jearldene's bassinet. Falene, Patsy, and I slept in the bunk beds during the night, while the three young men worked the graveyard shift at the factory. They'd come home in the morning and take our places for their turn, sleeping during the day while I was at school. Once Phyllis came along, my parents moved the bassinet into their room, and Jearldene was upgraded to a crib.

At the time, there was no commerce of any kind in Goodyear. Its development was happening so fast, and it would take a while for businesses not related to aircraft to catch up. The unincorporated area was divided into four parts by the intersection of two paved two-lane roads. Litchfield Road ran north to south, and Yuma Road ran east to west. (If you headed west along Yuma Road, you'd go past cotton fields, into the desert, and on to the White Tank Mountains. Head south on Litchfield Road past undeveloped land for a quarter of a mile, across the railroad tracks, and on to Buckeye Road to State Highway Route 85.)

In the southwest corner was the factory and airfield/landing-strip, occupying approximately 160 acres. In the northwest corner, there was an uncultivated forty-acre field with a giant cottonwood tree on the north bank of the irrigation ditch running parallel to Yuma Road. This parcel was awaiting construction of housing, if the need eventually arose. In the southeast corner were forty acres of flat-roof, single-story apartments and a community center. Our forty-acre subdivision was in the northeast corner. Just north of us was another forty acres of uncultivated farmland, which would be developed if needed by the factory. Until then, it was a playground for me and my buddies. If we needed to visit the doctor's office, the bank, a small commercial area, or the swimming pool, we'd have to travel past four miles of cotton fields to get to the city of Litchfield Park.

The nearest town was Avondale, approximately a half-mile to the east. Avondale consisted of a post office, a small country store, and a service station. And a bar—besides us, there were very few Mormons. (A little over a year after we moved there, a grocery store and a drugstore with a soda fountain would be added at the crossroads of our forty-acre site.) In the mornings, the other schoolchildren and I walked through alfalfa fields along a worn shortcut path from our Goodyear housing to Avondale Elementary School.

As far as another move and another school went, Goodyear was a pleasant surprise. I had boys my own age to play with, and I could just be a boy, rather than Grandpa's helper. Don't get me wrong; I loved helping Grandpa and enjoyed the times that I lived with my grandparents. But it was nice to just be a kid.

MONKEYING AROUND

With so many kids around, all of whom were newly arrived just like me, it was easy to make friends. Early on in the fourth grade, I was showing off at recess, trying to impress some students who were playing on the monkey bars. I climbed up and hung upside down from one of the bars by my knees. No big deal, was the consensus. Everyone could do that. But could I hang by my feet?

Well, you don't know unless you try. I managed to hang by the tops of my feet for nearly five seconds before falling off the monkey bars, headfirst. Naturally, I extended my arms to catch myself, and I ended up breaking my left arm below the elbow. Better that than my teeth.

In those days, the anesthesia used for putting someone under was ether. At the doctor's office, the doctor placed a large gauze pad over my nose and mouth, then dripped ether on the gauze.

Three . . . two . . . one . . .

While I was under, I had a strange dream, one that was weird enough for me to remember all these decades later. There was a big valentine-style heart with a long plank going through it. I was sitting on one end of the plank, and a girl, my friend Hana, was sitting on the other end. We were spinning around and around and around with a sound of *woooop! woooop! woooop!* at every rotation.

I woke up with a groggy head and a plaster of paris cast on my arm. Unlike the time I was run over by a car, my parents were able to pay the hospital bill without too much worry, thanks to my dad's new job.

Being unable to use my left arm didn't slow me down. About four weeks after the monkey-bar accident, I was playing around on South Mountain and slipped. I slid down the mountainside, pinning my left arm under my chest as I did. The rough rocky ground peeled a fair amount of the plaster of paris and gauze off my cast.

I was afraid to show my parents, but my mom just sighed and took me back to the doctor, who simply applied some more gauze and plaster of paris. That evening, I heard my dad grumbling. "The next time," he said, "I'll buy a box of plaster of paris and a roll of gauze and fix it myself. Save a hell of a lot of money, too."

A NEW YEAR'S BONFIRE

That Christmas, new buddies Billy and Ron, Ron's older brother, Ted, and I got a bright idea about how to make some money. For ten cents per tree, we would come over on New

Year's Day and haul off the old Christmas tree. There being no copy machines in those days, we handmade our own notices, and we knocked on the front door of every house in the subdivision two days after Christmas.

Once our client roster was established, we put my wagon and Ron's wagon into service. The brothers took one side of the street, and Billy and I took the other side. Down the blocks we wheeled our wagons, loading them as high as we could, then tying the trees down and hauling them to the vacant field north of the subdivision. There we made a huge pile of spent Christmas trees. I didn't keep count, but I can tell you we got trees from at least half of the subdivision's 150 houses, and that the pile was way over our heads.

We waited a couple of days to light our bonfire. The wintertime humidity in Arizona is exceptionally low, and the trees were very dry. Still, just to be sure, we wadded up old newspapers and stuffed them under some bottom branches.

When I struck a match and touched it to a crumpled newspaper, the trees exploded into a giant fireball. It was essentially one great big pile of kindling, after all. It happened so fast that I didn't even have time to take a step backward, and the fireball singed my eyelashes, eyebrows, and the front of my hair. I'm lucky it didn't do worse, even luckier that it didn't set the whole of Goodyear on fire. My parents were pretty tolerant of my shenanigans, but I think that would have been too much.

The next year we would get smart and use a long stick with a rag tied to the end to start the fire. And we would draw a crowd.

DOING OUR PART

With the war in full swing, the US government was putting out propaganda to make citizens feel that we were vital to the war effort, that we were doing our part to help win the war. This included not complaining about the rationing.

We now had ration books for tires and gasoline. Every motor vehicle had to display a gasoline sticker in the lower passenger's-side corner of the windshield to purchase gas. There were six different kinds; the A sticker was the most common and meant three to four gallons of gas a week. The B sticker was for driving deemed essential to the war effort, such as industrial war workers, who got eight gallons. An M sticker was for motorcycles, T for trucks, and X for VIPs. The C sticker was guaranteed unlimited gasoline, granted to emergency workers, doctors, military personnel, firefighters, farmworkers, and mail delivery vehicles. In fact, gas wasn't what they were really rationing—the main purpose of the restrictions on gas was to conserve tires.

The Japanese had conquered the prime rubber-producing nations of Malaya and the Dutch East Indies by March 1942, eliminating 91 percent of America's rubber supply.[3] Since cargo ships were needed for military purposes, the ability to import rubber from South America was reduced, which meant that tires were difficult to obtain. You had to get government permits to buy new ones, and to get the permit, you had to show that your tires were worn down to the treads. The "enough tread to touch Lincoln's head on a penny" test wasn't enough; if the tires were four ply, meaning four layers of threads, two of the layers had to be showing. Because of

---

3.   Sarah Sundin, "Make It Do – Tire Rationing in World War II," Sarah's Blog (blog), December 27, 2016, http://www.sarahsundin.com/make-it-do-tire-rationing-in-world-war-ii/.

this, people resorted to covering holes with a "rubber boot," a six-inch-long piece of rubber with a couple of layers of tread that fit inside the tire. Every driver kept a tool kit with tire irons, a jack, an inner tube patching kit, a tire pump, and tire boots in their trunk.

We also had ration stamps for food, including sugar, jam, coffee, tea, meat, tea, biscuits, breakfast cereals, butter, cheese, eggs, lard, milk, and canned and dried fruit. My family was lucky in that Grandpa's farm was only an hour's drive away. We got all the meat, lard, milk, and eggs we needed without having to use our ration stamps. No one in our house drank coffee, so that wasn't an issue. As for a sweetener, my uncle Grant had a large bee farm, and my folks would buy honey by the five-gallon can. We sweetened most everything with honey. Because of our access to these food essentials, we had a lot of leftover food stamps to trade with our neighbors for gas stamps.

Doing our part also consisted of us students lining up once a week to buy war stamps from the teacher. Stamps were 10¢, 25¢, 50¢, or $1, and we pasted them in our stamp books. When we had enough stamps in our book to equal $18.75, we could trade them for a $25 war bond at the post office or bank. At the end of ten years, you could redeem them for their face value, at a profit of $6.25. My dad also got a $25 war bond with each of his Goodyear paychecks.

For a kid, ten years to wait to cash out might as well have been an eternity. A more tangible way to help the war effort was through cultivating victory gardens.

VICTORY GARDENS AND A MISSING FRIEND

Dad had dug up a third of our backyard in order to plant vegetables and a plum tree, an apricot tree, and a peach tree.

That was our at-home victory garden. At school, we used a field donated by a local farmer. Every fourth- through eighth-grade student had a strip of land approximately two feet by twenty-five feet, plus seeds given to us by the school. Each row was wide enough to plant on both sides, making fifty feet worth of vegetables.

Hana, a Japanese American classmate, sat at the desk in front of me and had the garden next to mine. She was a soft-spoken girl, but it was easy to get her to giggle. I liked teasing her. You might call it fourth-grade flirting, though I would have vehemently denied it if you had said so back then. During recess, it wouldn't have been unusual to see me pushing her in a swing or the two of us sliding down the slide together. I liked being around her, and I was happy to help her plant her garden. We were friends.

One day, she wasn't at her desk. She wasn't there the next day either. "Where's Hana?" I asked the teacher on the third day, after the final bell had rung. Students were filing past us, shoving each other, calling out to one another, laughing. "Is she out sick?"

"No, Herb," the teacher said. "Hana and her family have been interned."

I had no idea what she was talking about. "What's 'interned'?" I asked.

The teacher sighed. "It's like a concentration camp."

I didn't know what that was either.

"We are at war with Japan," the teacher explained. "Hana's family is Japanese, and they could be helping our enemy. They have been taken to the Indian reservation, where they will live for a while."

I still didn't understand. Hana's dad worked at Goodyear, making airplanes to *fight* the Japanese. He wasn't helping them. *She* certainly wasn't helping them. Hana was just a kid! And she was my friend, not my enemy. Many years later I would learn that there had been two internment camps in Arizona. Despite the local Native Americans' protests, more than thirteen thousand Japanese Americans were incarcerated at Gila River Relocation Center on the Gila River Indian Reservation, and more than seventeen thousand Japanese Americans at Poston Relocation Center on the Colorado River Indian Reservation. Many of the barracks were built by Del Webb, the same company that had built my family's home.

Then something else occurred to me. "If we intern Japanese people in America, why don't we intern German people in America? What if German people here are helping Germany?"

The teacher's mouth became a thin line. She shook her head. "Go outside and play" was all she said.

At home, I asked my mom the same question. Her answer was not satisfying, though it was revealing in a way I couldn't comprehend at the time. "German people look like us," Mom said. She must have noticed the skeptical look on my face, because she added, "It would be harder to find out who here is from Germany." I was unconvinced.

The next day, the teacher gave Hana's garden to me. They were side by side, after all, and she knew that Hana and I had worked together in planting. Dad's victory garden provided most of the vegetables we needed, so as Hana's garden bloomed, I loaded up the produce on my Radio Flyer wagon and took them door to door to sell. Though I would finish the fourth, fifth, and sixth grades at Avondale Elementary—my longest stint in one school—I would never see Hana again.

THE TWO-DOLLAR DONKEY

Ron and Billy, my co-arsonists in the Christmas Tree Bonfire Fiasco of 1942, and I were playing down by the railroad tracks one sunny Saturday morning at the start of fifth grade when we saw a humanlike shape and a horselike shape coming toward us along the tracks. As they got closer, the shapes became an old man leading a donkey by a rope around its neck. The donkey was wearing an old straw hat with a sweatband of false flowers.

Of course, we ran down to get a better look. The man let us pet it, then asked us if we wanted to buy the donkey. "Only ten dollars," he said.

We turned away so that we could empty our pockets and count our money. Combined, we could only come with two dollars plus a little change. The old man shrugged, took our money, and handed me the rope. "He's all yours," he said. Being nine and ten years old, we didn't know or think about getting a bill of sale, or confirming that the donkey was really his to sell.

Before concluding the transaction, the old man broke off a small limb from an oleander shrub and trimmed it down to about two feet long. "You'll want to tap his jaw on the opposite side of the way you want him to turn," the man said while demonstrating. "Tap the right side to make him go left, the left side to make him go right. You don't have to tap hard. Be nice to the donkey and only tap him very lightly. OK?" The three of us nodded. "Now, to get the donkey to go," the man continued, "kick him softly with your heels against his ribs. C'mon, I'll show you."

The man extended his hand and helped us get up on the donkey. I got on first, with Ron and Billy behind me. The old man slipped the rope off the donkey's neck and handed me the stick. "Just a little kick now," he said. I nudged the donkey with my heels, confident because of my experience riding Suzy-Q at milking time on my grandparents' farm. "Good," the old man said, watching while we got the hang of it. Finally satisfied, he tipped his hat in farewell and walked away while we rode off in the other direction.

My two-dollar donkey.

I had put the most money in the pot, so I took ownership of the donkey, whom we named Poncho. When we arrived at my family's driveway, I heard Falene's voice coming from behind the screen door. "Louise," she was shouting to my mom, "come quick! You have to see this. Herbie's on a donkey!"

Mom and Falene ran out the front door. Although Mom was excited to see us on the donkey, I wasn't sure how she was going to take the news that we owned it. Still, Mom was not a practical person, doing and saying things before thinking about the consequences (like the time she tied my little black-and-white pedal car to the back of our Model A Ford), so I wasn't too worried.

"Where are you going to keep it?" Falene asked.

Before I could come up with an answer, Mom blurted out, "We can keep the donkey in the backyard."

"Uh, Louise? He'll eat everything in the garden," Falene said. There was a pause. After a moment, Mom said, "We'll wait 'til your dad gets home."

The women went back inside, and Billy, Ron, Poncho, and I clip-clopped up the street to show Ron and Billy's mothers. Neither boy told their mom that they had contributed to the purchase; as a matter of fact, they told them that Poncho was *my* donkey. Well, in that case, I might as well make it official. We clip-clopped back to my house, where the other boys and the donkey waited outside while I got money out of a wooden Velveeta box hidden in a drawer so I could buy them out. Now I was the proud sole owner of a two-dollar donkey.

But I didn't mind sharing. We kept on riding, and when we got to the alfalfa field, it dawned on me that we'd found a better alternative to my family's backyard. Here he'd have alfalfa to eat and water to drink from the irrigation ditch, a happy donkey life in this pastoral setting. Before settling Poncho in, however, I'd have to see what Dad said.

Back at home, Ron and Billy took off and I found some rope, looped it around Poncho's neck, and tied him to the lawn chair swing next to the driveway. Then I went inside the house for lunch. While I was eating a bologna-and-Velveeta sandwich, Falene was doing dishes at the kitchen sink. Out of the blue, she gasped. I looked up, then raced over to the window to see what she was looking at.

Now, a donkey doesn't know a patch of grass from a gravel driveway, and he has no qualms about public urination. There he was, relieving himself with abandon, his penis—all eighteen inches of it—hanging out, dripping on the driveway. Falene, being something of a prude, came unglued. "Herbie," she yelled, "you get out there and make that donkey pull his big thing up so the neighbors can't see it!" I was laughing so hard that tears were running down my face. "Get out there, Herbie! We can't have a donkey in front of our house with his thing hanging down!"

Trying to suppress my giggles, I said, "That's . . . that's just . . . oh my gosh . . . that's just how donkeys pee, Falene."

Still laughing, I heard her say, "Phew, he's putting it back in where it belongs." I took a deep breath to collect myself. She continued, "You go on and take him out to the field when he needs to pee."

"How am I going to know when he needs to pee?" I asked. "He doesn't speak English, and I don't understand donkey talk."

When Dad got home and found out that I now owned a donkey, he started laughing and said, "Where did you get him?"

"I bought him with my own money."

Not a full answer, but apparently it was good enough to satisfy Dad, because he said, "Where are you going to keep him? And what are you going to feed him?"

"I'm going to keep him in the field with the alfalfa."

"I'm sure Goodyear owns that field to build on. For now, let's go see what we can do."

We found a spot where the donkey could reach the irrigation ditch and had enough reseeded alfalfa to eat, just as I'd planned. After he'd been watered and fed, I led him back home.

On the way, Dad and I had a little talk. "You own him, so you are responsible for him."

"Yeah, I know."

"He has to be exercised every day. If he poops in someone's yard or in the street, you have to clean it up. Understood?"

These are the types of things that little boys don't think about when they spontaneously buy a donkey. After a moment of weighing my options—and realizing that there were none—I said, "Sure, Dad."

When we got back to the house, my dad went to his shop in the garage. He found an iron bar about three-quarters of an inch in diameter, lit up his welding torch, and heated and pounded the rod on the anvil until he made an eye on the end to tie the rope through. He handed me the rod and got out the sledgehammer, and off we went to make the home for the donkey official.

A few days later, when I went out to the field to ride him, Poncho was gone and so were the rod and the rope. I spent most of the day looking for him, riding my bicycle up and down the streets and around the field, but to no avail. That donkey was nowhere to be found. Perhaps the old man who sold him to us came back and got him.

THE FLAMING ARROW

One of the benefits of our living in Goodyear was that I had lots of boys my age to play with. This was ideal in terms of entertainment, but not so wonderful in terms of sensible decision making. It is inevitable that a group of boys—especially any group of boys that *I* would want to be friends with—will get up to no good.

One day, a few of us came up with the bright idea of having a bow-and-arrow fight, our 1940s version of paintball. Except instead of shooting each other with hard gelatin capsules filled with paint, we wanted to use actual pointy metal arrows. You know, the kind that pierce skin and kill people.

Now, we weren't total idiots. We did realize the danger of using arrows. A brainstorming session ensued. What about cutting the sharpened point off the end? Nah, that would be too difficult, and it would take the fun out of it. What about putting cotton balls over the end of the arrow? We tried it, test shooting an arrow with a cotton ball taped over the end. When the padded arrow struck a tree, the pointy part went right through the cotton ball and into the trunk. Back to the drawing board. How about tying a cloth around it? I volunteered my T-shirt, ripping off a strip of cloth and tightly winding it around and over the tip. Now we had a new problem: the arrow was too heavy on the end and wouldn't go straight or as far. Foiled again.

Just before one of us would have to admit that perhaps a bow-and-arrow fight wasn't the world's best idea, one of the guys took the cloth-wrapped arrow and lit it on fire, then shot it up in the air. We watched in awe as it soared into the sky, the flames appearing to go out as it took on height. But apparently the cloth retained an ember or two throughout its flight—at least enough to ignite the dead grass we were standing in when it landed.

The fire spread fast. In a panic, we all started stomping the ground, lucky that the grass was short and not very thick. Even luckier, an irrigation ditch full of water created a barrier between our field and the adjacent cotton field, stopping the fire from spreading and saving us from getting into major trouble. Crisis averted yet again, not because of any intelligence or foresight on our part. Just pure damn luck.

COTTON PICKERS

The war in Europe had created a shortage of able-bodied men in the US, and Rosie the Riveter and her fellow—that is, female—patriots were called upon to fill in. This was an incredible opportunity for women who'd been barred from the workplace because of their gender; now, women who wanted to work outside of the home could. Not that they'd reached equal status—even though women's contribution was vital to the war effort, on average they were paid 50 percent less than their male counterparts.[4]

An ad for cotton pickers to replace the men who'd gone off to fight appeared on the bulletin board at the post office and caught Falene's eye. Jearl was now fighting in China, and here was a way for her to do her part, as well as make some money for the household. She managed to convince Mom to join her; they could make a lot of money, she said, at two dollars per hundred pounds.

---

4. "American Women in World War II," History.com (website), https://www.history.com/topics/world-war-ii/american-women-in-world-war-ii-1.

Though Mom and Falene had plenty of experience doing manual labor, neither had ever picked cotton, not even for their dad. Grandpa hired Native Americans from the Fort McDowell Indian Reservation, and usually twenty-five to thirty people worked at a time. If you were watching from a distance, it appeared that they were working quickly and easily. In reality, it came down to the number of pickers, not their speed, that filled the cotton wagon.

Picking cotton is hard work. Back then, an expert picker could pick three hundred pounds of "clean" cotton in a day. That meant the cotton balls would be free of the protective bolls that hold them to the plants, as well as other limbs and leaves. (Cotton gins would often reject cotton if it was "dirty," and the worker would have to comb through the cotton again to remove the offending plant material.) One hundred pounds of clean cotton, or approximately 45,000 bolls, yields twenty-four to thirty-eight pounds of pure cotton fibers after ginning (removing the seeds). Mom and Falene would have to pick 45,000 bolls each to earn two bucks.

I think Mom and Falene thought they were going to be able to pick a couple hundred pounds of cotton, make some quick cash, call it a day. I went with them to give it a try, too.

Even now, whenever I put on a cotton T-shirt or a cotton pair of socks, I remember that day out in the cotton fields. If you've never picked cotton, it's hard to imagine just how much (wo)manpower goes into every fiber. I can tell you from experience: it's a lot. Coaxing the fibers from the boll is not as easy as it looks, and if you're not careful the points on the end of the boll can draw blood. And even a big cotton ball weighs almost nothing.

Cotton bolls, both before and after being picked.

After about four hours of picking, Mom and Falene had had enough. They turned in their tote sacks and went home while I kept going, picking a total of sixteen pounds of cotton that day. The thirty-two cents I made jingled in my pocket as I dragged my exhausted body home. I don't know how much Falene or Mom made, but I can tell you, it certainly wasn't folding money.

THE ICE TRUCK

To run out of ice, especially during an Arizona summer, was the equivalent to a power failure today. Even when it was well stocked, the internal temperature of the icebox was probably not much below 50 degrees Fahrenheit, meaning ice cream would melt if left in too long. (I always did my part in eating all the ice cream as soon as my mom or dad brought it home from the store.) Of course, we didn't have air-conditioning, so when the temperature climbed, often the only relief was a cold drink. But if the ice supply was too low, my mom would not let us chip off chunks to put in our Kool-Aid or occasional soda.

Having an icebox required much more work than with today's refrigerators and freezers, starting with the ice deliveries. I remember an old heavy-duty truck with no doors on the cab so the driver could slip in and out quickly. A big wooden enclosure lined with two-inch-thick sheets of cork insulation, tall enough for a man to stand up inside, occupied the bed of the truck and had a heavy canvas flap that tied in the center or off to the side. When the truck stopped in front of our house, we kids would run to the back and begin our search for ice chips. Sometimes there would already be nice ice chips available for the taking. Other times, the kids on the previous block would have taken them all. In that case, we would have to wait while the ice man climbed into the bed of the truck, pulled his trusty ice pick out of its little leather holster on his belt, and, with a few well-aimed jabs, broke a fifty- or twenty-five-pound block from one of the two big hundred-fifty-pound blocks and slid it to the rear. Then he'd jump down to the pavement, a leather or burlap cover over his shoulder, and stoop so that he could slide the ice off the truck bed and onto his shoulder. He would stand and head for the back door of the house, balancing the ice with one hand, leaving the other one free to open the door. There was no knocking or pausing at the door—every second counted. He would just open it wide with the loud announcement "Ice man!"

Everyone would scatter so that he could go directly to the icebox and place the ice on its designated galvanized shelf at the top. Air would circulate around the ice and back down to the lower shelves where the food was kept. As the ice melted, the water drained away from the ice to keep the rate of melting from increasing, into a pipe that went out the bottom of the icebox, where an average-size dishpan collected it.

My mom tended to worry about the drip pan. Depending on the temperature in the house, the drip pan would fill in about twelve hours. The pan was always the last thing to be checked before bed at night, and it was the responsibility of the first person in the kitchen in the morning to empty it. I remember many times coming into the kitchen in my bare feet early and stepping into a layer of cold water that had spread across the kitchen floor during the night. If my mother arrived first to find this same scenario, she would announce for all the house to hear, "We forgot the drip pan last night. Somebody get the mop."

THE KÜHNS

My fifth-grade teacher, Mrs. Kühn, was very young and very pretty. I had a crush on her from day one. She liked me, too; I don't know if it was the daisy that I picked and gave to her the second day of school, or if it was because I readily volunteered to run errands for her, but soon I became the teacher's pet.

My crush started dying, however, when I met her husband, our science teacher. It died once and for all when I returned to the classroom during recess to hang up my coat and found Mrs. Kühn smoking. She panicked. "Don't tell anyone. OK, Herb?" she pleaded. I promised I wouldn't, and I never did. Not until now, anyway.

Mr. Kühn was my all-time favorite teacher. Ever since I could remember, I had been interested in how things worked, from car engines to milk separators. I was always asking, reading, thinking, or experimenting, something my family encouraged. In a practical sense, you had to know how things worked on a farm so that you could fix them when they broke.

Mr. Kühn had a fun, hands-on approach to teaching. He even taught biology that way. Instead of making us memorize the parts of a grasshopper's leg out of a book, we would catch grasshoppers and examine them through magnifying glasses. He also had a tarantula in a terrarium, which I eventually worked up the nerve to hold, a great way for proving my manliness and teasing girls. Every week, I could hardly wait for the half day of science class, a curriculum that included physical science, earth science, astronomy, and biology. I became a science sponge and a science seeker. If I saw Mr. Kühn during recess, I would leave whatever game I was involved in so that I could go and talk to him about science. He seemed to appreciate my enthusiasm.

One recess, I asked Mr. Kühn why it was hot in the summer and cold in the winter.

"It's the way the Earth is tilted toward the sun," he replied. "In summer, the Earth is tilted toward the sun, and in winter it's tilted away from the sun." I must have looked puzzled, because he continued, "OK, you are going to be the sun and I'm going to be the Earth. You stand straight up right here and pretend you are hot. Now, I'm going to be the Earth, and I'm going to stand at an angle as I walk around you, the sun." He leaned to his right, toward me. "What part of me is closer to the sun?"

"Your right side."

"OK, imagine if you lived on my right ear." He started to slowly walk around me, keeping the same lean to the right. "If my right ear is close to the sun, is it hotter or colder than if you lived on, say, my left elbow?"

I thought for a second. "Hotter!"

"So would it be summer or winter on my right ear?"

"Summer!"

He continued walking clockwise, maintaining the tilted body position. He stopped on the side of me opposite of where he'd started. "Now, is my right ear pointed toward you or away from you?"

"Away."

"So is it hotter or colder, summer or winter?"

"It's winter and it's cold!"

"Right on!"

Mr. Kühn and I discussed the Earth, the sun, and how the seasons change until the bell rang. By the time fifth grade was over, my commitment to becoming a scientist had cemented in my mind. In college, I would major in physical sciences, with a minor in biology and earth science, and I would remember Mr. Kühn's style of teaching when I became a teacher. From him I learned that it doesn't matter how well funded a school is, or if it has the most up-to-date technology or the most prestige. It always comes back to the teachers and their love of teaching. I would use whatever I could to spark the same interest Mr. Kühn had sparked in me: visual effects, 3-D models, dramatic demonstrations, relevant analogies. And, of course, like him I would always welcome questions and encourage curiosity.

HOT FEET

My dad's youngest brother, Ed, was a year and a half older than I was; he was the one with whom I'd gotten in big trouble after breaking the log crane back when we lived in Coconino National Forest. Grandpa Bryce had died in 1937 and Grandma Bryce in 1939, and he'd been living with his oldest sister, Beulah, ever since. Occasionally he'd spend the summer with us, and the June after I finished fifth grade he arrived on our doorstep. Even though he was really my uncle, to me he was like a big brother. I loved it when he was around.

Shortly after Ed came to Goodyear, he and I took off one morning to go swimming. The nearest public swimming pool was in Litchfield Park, four miles north of where we lived. When I went with my buddies, we rode our bikes, but since Ed didn't bring his bike, we decided to walk. We left wearing our bathing suits and carrying a towel. You'll notice that I didn't mention shoes. That's because I wasn't so great at thinking ahead, and this case was no exception. We left home barefoot, a comfortable walk in the early morning temperature of merely the high eighties.

We had a wonderful day playing in the swimming pool. One of our favorite—and stupidest—games was called "bombing the submarine." Ed would dive down and swim along the bottom of the deep end of the pool, and I would jump off the three-meter tower, feet first, and try to land on his back. Then we'd switch.

In the midafternoon, when the tips of our fingers and toes were thoroughly wrinkled and our shoulders were pink, we decided to go home. By this time the temperature had climbed maybe 20 degrees or so, and the sun had been blazing down on the blacktop for hours. One foot on the road resulted in a screech of pain and the knowledge that it was now too hot to walk home barefoot.

Walking on the side of the road wasn't an option either, because it was lined with bullheads, an invasive ground cover plant that has seeds with two thorns pointing out like the horns on a bull's head. Those thorns are hard and long enough to puncture a bicycle tire, not to mention the softer skin of human feet.

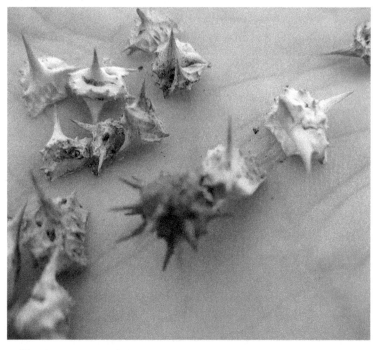

Bullheads, sometimes called goat heads.

"Why don't we throw our towels, then run and jump on them?" I suggested. We gave it a try—throw the towel, run, step on the towel, pause to give our feet a break, repeat—and discovered that a dry towel would kind of flutter and not go very far. At the rate we were going, it would take us a million years to get home.

"What if we got our towels wet so that they'll be heavier and go farther?" Ed proposed. That did work better; we could throw the towels ten or fifteen feet, then run as fast as we could on our burning feet. Soon we discovered another problem: the heat of the road quickly dried the towels.

By this time, we were far enough down the road to not want to admit the weakness of our plan. I'm sure stubbornness had something to do with it, too. So we figured out a solution that somehow combined the *worst* of all options. To get the towels wet, we laid them down and shuffled across the six feet of bullheads on the side of the road to get to the irrigation ditch, where we could soak them again. This took an additional one million years.

After throwing and running and walking through thorns over and over again for a mile or so, a woman driving toward Goodyear took pity on us and gave us a ride. Moral of the story: stop and think before leaving the house without shoes.

HOW NOT TO IMPRESS YOUR TEACHER

Just as some teachers teach by inspiring us and bringing out our best, some teachers teach by modeling what *not* to do and what *not* to be. My sixth-grade teacher was one such anti-role model. I do not remember his name, nor do I want to. He does not deserve to be remembered. But for simplicity's sake, I will call him Mr. Tobacco Stain.

Mr. Tobacco Stain was a gross and uncouth man, the opposite of Mr. and Mrs. Kühn in every respect. There's one telling scene that has stuck in my mind: Mrs. Kühn and I were standing on the sidewalk talking when Mr. Tobacco Stain walked up, interrupted without apology, and started talking to Mrs. Kühn. During this brief conversation, he placed his finger against the side of his nose and blew snot onto the grass. Didn't say a word about it. This was at a time when you went out of your way to open doors for women, gave up your seat to them, kept your language clean. I'd been taught to treat women with the utmost respect. Obviously, Mr. Tobacco Stain needed to get some lessons from Miss Manners.

He also chewed tobacco and had black tobacco stains in the corners of his mouth. He kept a spit can in the top right-hand corner of his desk, which he would use every now and then while teaching. I don't know how he got away with blatantly chewing tobacco when Mrs. Kühn had been so embarrassed to be caught smoking.

Along with the spit can, he also kept the Bible on his desk. He taught science, yet the religious text trumped fact, and he often made mistakes or, it seemed to me, simply made things up. I, as Mr. Know-It-All, would try to correct him in front of the class, which he did not take kindly.

One afternoon, he tried to teach us that the sun went around the Earth. I'd spent that very enjoyable recess with Mr. Kühn learning the exact opposite, but when I brought up the fact that the Earth goes around the sun, Mr. Tobacco Stain was incensed.

"It's in the Bible," he said, scorn in his voice. "Joshua commanded the Earth to stand still, and the sun stood still until the battle was won." Then he picked up his Bible and read Joshua, chapter 12, verses 12 and 13.

I waited for him to finish before saying, "That was before people knew about science. They didn't know that the Earth goes around the sun when they wrote that."

"If the Bible says so, it's true," Mr. Tobacco Stain said, "because the Bible was written by the hand of God."

"It was not," I argued. "That book was written by Joshua. That's why it's called 'Joshua.' All the books in the Old Testament were written by prophets, not God. Don't you know anything about who wrote the Bible?"

That comment was the straw that broke the camel's back. Mr. Tobacco Stain started toward me, yelling, "You get out of my class and never come back!" over and over. It was clear that he'd had enough; I stood up and rushed out of there.

I sighed with relief as the door closed behind me. Now I had another problem. I couldn't go home, because if I did, I'd have to explain to Mom what had happened. I couldn't go to the office, because if someone asked what had happened, it would come out that I'd talked back to a teacher. I was smarter than I had been as a little first grader and knew that leaving school entirely might cause more problems than it was worth. But I had to go somewhere.

Saved by the bell. At least, that's what I thought when the recess bell rang. Doors up and down the hallway opened, and kids came pouring out. I joined the flow toward the playground. Outside, I saw a group was gathering to play softball, so that's where I headed. On the way, I ran into Mr. Kühn. I knew I could trust him with this problem, and maybe get some advice as to what I should do.

I was in the middle of telling Mr. Kühn what had happened when Mr. Tobacco Stain approached, a murderous look on his face. Emboldened by Mr. Kühn's sympathy, I decided to poke the bear. This would turn out to be one of my worst decisions yet.

"My teacher is so dumb," I said, "that he doesn't even know who wrote the Bible!"

Mr. Tobacco Stain must have heard me, as I'd intended, because he picked up a bat and headed my way, swearing and yelling and slowly swinging it back and forth. I took the hint, turned, and started running away, picking up my pace as he caught up with me. With a jolt I realized, *If he catches me, he's gonna kill me.* That's where the thinking stopped and survival mode kicked in.

I stopped running, turned around, and tackled Mr. Tobacco Stain. We hit the ground, and the bat flew out of his hand. I sat on top of him and pounded him in the face as hard and fast as I could. Full of adrenaline, I didn't notice a group of teachers running toward us to break up the fight.

Mr. Kühn pulled me off, and three other teachers held Mr. Tobacco Stain down, trying to calm him before letting him up. Mr. Kühn put his arm around my shoulders and, talking softly to me like you would a spooked horse, walked me to the principal's office.

"Sit here," he said, gently pushing me into a seat. He knocked on the door and went in, closing it behind him.

I don't know what Mr. Kühn and the principal talked about while I sat there in a daze. It seemed like they were in there forever. Finally, the door opened and Mr. Kühn came out.

"Go on in," he said. "I gotta get to class."

By this time, the adrenaline had worn off and fear had taken its place. I had punched a teacher! Many times! In the face!

"Take a seat, young man," the principal said, gesturing to a chair in front of his broad wooden desk. He then proceeded to lecture me on respectful behavior and reactivity, nothing I didn't already know. "I'm going to have to call your mother to come and take you home."

"Yes, sir."

"You are to stay home until next Monday."

"Yes, sir."

I didn't know what was coming next, but my suspension gave me plenty of time to think about it. Would they send me back to Mr. Tobacco Stain? I'd seen the gleam in his eye and had no doubt that he'd try to use that baseball bat if given a chance.

For the rest of the week and through the weekend, I behaved myself, even going so far as to be nice to my sisters. My dad and I had a long discussion about respecting grown-ups, even if they don't deserve it, and how fighting never solves anything. My parents surprised me by not punishing me. Wondering what would happen on Monday was punishment enough.

When I returned to school after the weekend, the sixth grade had a new teacher.

Mr. Kühn and the other teachers had come to my defense. They'd seen him with the bat and witnessed how he was the one who'd chased me. So even though I'd tackled him, he was held at fault. He was an adult, after all.

I wonder if the principal had been looking for an excuse to get rid of Mr. Tobacco Stain, even though male teachers were hard to find during that time because of the war. Whatever the reason, I was not the only student who was glad to be free of Mr. Tobacco Stain and his nasty spit can. Our new teacher taught that the Earth goes around the sun.

This was the first of the three fights I had in my life. It convinced me that I had to remain in control of myself. There is always a better way.

HERBSY NERDSY HAD A GREAT FALL

There was a monster of a cottonwood tree growing in the big field on the northwest corner of Goodyear, next to the irrigation ditch. It was at least forty-five feet high, and it happened to be in the direct line of the flight path to the Goodyear Factory landing field. If a cargo airplane was landing to the south or taking off to the north, it had to fly over the tree at less than one hundred feet.

You would think that kids building a tree house would take this into account. But my buddies and I were so focused on the utter perfection of that tree, how it cried out for a tree house, and so we didn't look at the big picture. You may have noticed a pattern here—foresight just wasn't my thing.

It took about a week for us to scavenge the materials needed. We decided to build our tree house close to the top of the tree, a height at which we could play in private and also keep out girls. We nailed in place a couple of ladders from one big limb to another and rigged a pulley system to get the boards and other materials up.

We hauled and hammered at a fast clip, and soon the platform that would be the floor of the tree house was complete, well secured to two big limbs. Or, at least I thought it was—until I got an unforgettable lesson in engineering.

Ron and Billy were on the ground getting boards ready to be pulled up, and I was standing on the platform surveying our handiwork, when a four-engine cargo plane flew over the top of the tree to land on the runway. The prop wash was so strong that it blew those two limbs apart, unhooking the nails and the platform with them. The platform fell out from under me, and all of a sudden I was standing on air. Then I fell, too.

This is another instance in which a guardian angel must have been paying attention. Instead of falling straight to the ground, where I would likely have broken every bone in my body, I dropped onto a medium-size limb, my head and arms hanging over one side and my legs and feet hanging over the other side. I grunted as the wind was knocked out of me, but the limb had enough give to slow me down without really injuring me.

Then I heard a cracking sound. The limb started to break under my weight, but I was able to ease myself off and climb down before it broke completely. I walked away with a few—well, considerably more than a few—scrapes and bruises but in one piece.

We were lucky that I was the only one in the tree at that time. This incident scared all of us so badly that we abandoned the project, leaving a pile of boards and a busted tree house floor at the base of the trunk, and walked silently home.

Looking back, I'm surprised that I'm still alive. Who knows why God has allowed me to escape death more than once. Years ago, when I told my wife, Gloria, this story, she said, "I know why. He was saving you for me!"

"There couldn't have been a better reason," I said. I sure loved that gal.

CHAPTER 7

A Return to Mesa: 1945–1947

The beginning of the end of World War II was on June 6, 1944, when the Allied troops stormed the beaches of the French town of Normandy. Germany officially surrendered on May 8, 1945. That August the United States dropped two atomic bombs on the Japanese cities of Hiroshima and Nagasaki, killing hundreds of thousands of people both instantly and eventually from radiation poisoning. Japan signed the documents of surrender on September 2, officially ending the war.

Tens of millions of people had died during the past six years; many more had experienced terrible hardship and loss. The world had seen the horrors wrought by combining new technology with age-old bigotry and greed. Now, all across the world, we celebrated and hoped for peace.

At twelve years old, I'd lived half of my life during wartime. I suppose that's the case for most people—unfortunately, every era has its war.

Without the demand of military airplanes, the Goodyear factory lost its contract and so closed down production. Almost all of Mom's family moved back to Mesa, regrouping in the town near where they'd grown up. My mom was happy to get back to Mormon country, to be surrounded by her fellow Mormons and the culture of the Mormon Church.

Bud, the oldest brother of Falene's husband, Jearl, offered Dad a job making concrete roofing tiles. Bud owned land west of Mesa, which he'd subdivided into lots for building houses. We rented one of those houses, located in the district for Alma School and about six miles from Grandpa's new farm. I'm sure that they didn't consider my changing schools again when making the decision to move; Dad's employment always had to come first.

NEW HOME, NEW HORMONES

In many ways, the seventh grade was a calmer period of my childhood. I'd had some near-death experiences, learned some lessons, developed a basic understanding of who I was and what my interests were. But, like many soon-to-be-teenage boys, my hormones had started to kick in. Suddenly I was more interested in hanging out with girls than with my pals. Don't get me wrong—I still liked playing football, soccer, and baseball. After practice, however, I would rather spend time with a girl, holding hands or even sneaking an occasional kiss. That was enough for me. These kisses were wholly chaste, not the passionate lip-chewing kind you see in movies.

I lived at the edge of farming country, and my modes of transportation were walking or biking, both of which had their advantages. Walking allowed for hand-holding while strolling through grassy fields. Because of the examples of my romantic father and grandfather, I knew to stop and pick a wildflower for the girl I was with. My bicycle, on the other hand, was better for traveling longer distances to the movies, out to a good swimming hole, or to Upton's Ice Cream Store for a cone. This was casual and not considered dating, though it did allow for a little romance. The girl would sit sidesaddle on the crossbar, and if she slid back and I leaned forward, then we could ride close.

Helen and I figured out a way to ride cheek to cheek as well. Helen was Mormon and lived a couple of houses south of me; she was a year younger and seemed to have a case of the hormones, too. As the youngest of four daughters, with a widowed mother who held a long, loose string on her girls, Helen was always game for some adventure.

She and another neighborhood girl, Ann, who was my age, both lived nearby and both seemed to enjoy spending time with me. Ann was Catholic and lived just across a small diversion canal that ran north and south next to our property. I tied a rope on a limb of the large cottonwood tree on the bank across the canal and installed a post with a cleat to secure the rope on our side of the canal, and whenever I wanted to visit Ann I could swing over and swing back. Her dad did not appreciate the convenience of that. She was an only child of stern parents, and her father didn't buy into Ann and me spending a lot of time together one-to-one. Of course, nothing makes young love more exciting than the disapproval of parents.

For the next few years, until I met and married my first wife, Joyce, in 1954, I would continue this pattern of casual dating. I suppose some people might think that dating more than one person at a time is a recipe for disaster, or that you have to be dishonest or caddish to do so. For me, it came down to the simple fact that I preferred hanging out with girls—the interactions were always more interesting than those with my more-macho guy friends, who tended to brag or talk sports and not much else. Women, I've found, are more likely to be able to carry on a decent conversation, and that is more important to me than anything. For the record, I always treated every girl and woman I knew with respect. As long as all parties are straightforward and polite and truthful, friendship mixed with a little romance can be a lot of fun.

TWO THUMPS

And so I started seventh grade at Alma School, the same school I'd gone to for the first half of second grade and the second half of third grade. Though this wasn't a completely new school to me, it represented my eighth school move.

Soon after the school year began, my classmate Philip was riding on the back of his brother's scooter on the highway. I was not given the details; all I know is that somehow he fell off, and the car that had been driving behind them ran over and killed him.

His mother wanted six of his classmates to be pallbearers. I was chosen not because he and I were best friends but because of my size. There were still a couple of years before I'd reach my full adult height (five feet eight), but for a seventh grader I was tall, as well as strong from all the manual labor I'd done.

Outside the church, we six boys, dressed in our Sunday best, gathered around the coffin, then counted to three and picked it up at the same time, each of us placing it on a shoulder.

It was lighter than I'd imagined it would be. The ceremony was held in a chapel on the second floor, and as we ascended the stairs, the coffin slanted and the body slid down, the feet hitting the end of the coffin with an audible thud. I can tell you, that is not a nice sound. Once we got inside, the funeral director had to open the lid in order to pull Philip back into position before the congregants filed in.

We knew what was coming, but there was no way around it. After the service, when we were carrying the coffin back down the stairs to put into the hearse, the body again slid down with a thud. That time, I think the funeral director just left him as is, since the coffin would not be opened again. His mom gave each of us a little white Bible to remember her son by.

I wasn't fazed by this early death. For one, I didn't know Philip very well. And two, I was comfortable with the fact that animals die, humans die; it was all part of the natural course of life. Anyway, we didn't talk about it, not at home and not at school. As far as Mesa was concerned, grief counseling hadn't been invented yet. In fact, I didn't hear the word "trauma" until the late 1960s or early '70s, when more people started being vocal about mental health.

Because I grew up within a culture that accepted death without much fuss and, for whatever reason, I've never had trouble moving on after loss, later in life I had a difficult time comprehending why a school would spend thousands of dollars to bring counselors in after a student's death or other tragedy. It's only recently that I've come to understand the value of mulling over a moment, of revisiting the past.

GRANDPA IS DEFINITELY THE MARRYING KIND

In 1946, Grandpa broke up with his third wife. Yes, you read that right: his *third* wife.

Grandpa had remarried four months after Grandma died in 1942. Even though Grandpa had sold the family farm in order to buy a brass casket in which to bury Grandma and pay the burial fees, and all but one of their kids were grown and on their own (Maxine was twelve), someone needed to take over the work she'd done. Every pair of hands was essential to running a farm, and Grandma and Grandpa had each had set duties. (In some ways, too, Grandpa was just an old-fashioned guy—I doubt he washed a single dish in his entire life.) Lula Iva Evans, a widow and the woman who became Grandpa's second wife, could take over that labor and in return get the support she and her children needed on their farm. I suspect that it also had to do with sex along with companionship. The church frowned upon premarital relations, and so people often got married for the sake of fulfilling that particular basic need.

For these reasons, Grandpa married and moved in with Lula. He'd assumed he was getting some kind of carbon copy of his first wife, which, obviously, was a foolish assumption. It soon became apparent that this was not a good match, and the two went their separate ways within a year. Almost immediately, he married and moved in with Lola Nichols, in 1944. Together they bought 160 acres of farmland outside of Mesa. Her children, Lawrence, Shirley, Andrew, and Gene, came with her.

Lola was the polar opposite of Grandma, as well as twenty years younger, a 180-degree departure from the woman who'd raised me during my earliest years. Lola was her own person and outspoken—with her you always knew where you stood, no ifs, ands, or buts about it. She probably would have fit in just as well in New York City as in small-town Arizona. The strange thing was, Lola and Grandpa were true companions as well as spouses, a rare occurrence that Grandpa lucked into not once but twice in his life. They had respect and passion for one another, and they got along beautifully. That is, until Lola's ex-husband showed up.

A DENT AND A DIVORCE

Grandpa was standing there, waiting for Lola's ex-husband, Roy, to get out of his beat-up Dodge pickup, which he had parked with a scattering of gravel in back of the house. It was time for the afternoon milking, but the cows would have to wait.

As soon as Roy slammed the door, he was greeted with a loud "What the hell are you doing here?"

"I've come to pick up Lola and take her back to Yuma with me."

"There's no way in hell that's going to happen," Grandpa said, not moving an inch. "Get in the truck and get the hell out of here!"

Two of Roy and Lola's sons, fourteen-year-old Andrew and sixteen-year-old Lawrence, appeared on the scene. Lawrence had a baseball bat in his hand, which he nonchalantly swung back and forth as they approached. A few feet from their father, Lawrence positioned the bat on his right shoulder, as if he was ready to hit a home run, and Roy's head just might serve as the baseball. "You heard Mr. Herbert," Lawrence said. "Get the hell out of here."

"You can't talk to me that way," Roy said, eyeing the bat. "I'm your dad."

"The hell you are! You stopped being my dad the day you ran off with Rosa." Lawrence took a step closer to Roy. "Mr. Herbert is our dad now. Get your ass back in the truck and go back to Yuma, where you belong."

Roy shook his head and sighed, then took a final look at the baseball bat before retreating to the safety of his truck. He wasn't ready to call it quits, however, because he rolled down the window and stuck his head out. "I want to talk to Lola," he said.

Lawrence turned to Andrew. "Go in the house and make sure Mom stays there," he said, then walked over to the front of the truck and added a dent to the fender. Looking at his father, he said, "If you want to keep the windshield in one piece, you better get off this farm."

Roy finally realized it was going to be a solo trip back to Yuma. He turned the truck around and pushed the gas pedal to the floor. The spinning of rear tires and the spewing of dirt and gravel was his angry reply to Lawrence.

Soon we'd find out that Lola's daughter, Shirley, had heard that Rosa, her dad's girlfriend, had left Roy for a much younger man with a newer pickup. Shirley wrote to her dad, telling him that her mom missed him and was still in love with him and wanted to get back together. I have no idea what prompted her to take the matter into her own hands like that. Perhaps it was just wishful thinking. Or it could have been that Maxine, who was the same age as her new stepsister, had a group of good girlfriends and a bunch of boys fighting over her, while Shirley had neither. She might just have been lonely.

Roy should have realized that his chosen response would be like driving into a hornet's nest. A couple of days later, Lola called him to tell him to stay out of her life and never come back.

When Grandpa found out about this call, even though it was meant to finalize her split from Roy, he lost it. When two bullheaded people get their pride hurt, common sense goes out the window. The fight that followed lasted for several days and ended in a separation.

LIKE DRIVING A TRACTOR

Grandpa moved in with us after the breakup. He and Lola owned 160 acres together, and they agreed that she would continue to occupy the main house and he would live in a corner of their big property; first, however, he would have to build a house.

There was still work to be done on the farm, even though Grandpa was not currently living there. I'd just finished the seventh grade, so it was back to milking cows and mending fences for me, too. In the summertime, the morning routine—or, you might say, "the late-late-late-night routine"—consisted of getting up at 4:30 a.m. to drive the six miles to the farm and help Lola's two oldest boys, Lawrence and Andrew, milk the cows. Her youngest, Gene, fed and cared for the calves while we milked. (Even though he and I were the same age, he was three years behind me in school and was treated like a child, whereas I was always treated as someone older than I actually was.) When milking was over and the cows had been turned loose to graze, we headed to the house to eat the breakfast Lola had prepared. After breakfast, Lola's three boys, Grandpa, and I joined Talmage and Jearl to work on building Grandpa's house. As veterans of World War II, my two uncles were taking advantage of their G.I. Bill and, as college students, had the summer off.

One July dawn, the obnoxious sound of the alarm clock jittering across the bedside table let me know that it was four thirty and time to get up. I hit the alarm with a little more force than necessary, then sat up. Even though it was starting to get light outside, I was not at all ready to get out of bed. But those cows couldn't wait. I got dressed, splashed some water on my face, and went into the other room to see if Grandpa was ready. He was still in bed, looking like he'd spent all night on a torture rack. "Grandpa?" I said.

"My back is killing me," he said through clenched teeth. "You'll have to go by yourself and see that the cows get milked."

"What? How am I going to get there? I can't walk that far and get the milking done in time for the milk truck. What about Lawrence and Andrew? They're Lola's cows, too!"

"I want you to be there to see that it gets done and done right."

I sighed in frustration. "They won't do what I tell them to do," I said. "They're both older than me. They're in high school! Anyway, you haven't told me just how I'm supposed to get there. Should I wake up Mom or Dad to take me?"

"No, no, let them and your sisters sleep. You are going to drive my car."

"Grandpa, I can't drive your car. I'm only twelve! Are you crazy?"

"My back is killing me, and I'm not going to lie here arguing with you. You know how to drive the tractor."

"The tractor is at the farm."

"No, what I'm saying is, the car drives pretty much like the tractor. Go get the toilet plunger and bring it here."

"What? What do you want the plunger for?"

"Stop asking questions, we don't have time. I'm going to teach you how to shift gears." This all seemed nuts to me, but I got the plunger. "Sit in the chair next to the bed," Grandpa said, "and secure the plunger to the floor next to you in the same position as the gearshift in the car." I did as told while he gave me instructions. The shifting in his car was even simpler than other cars, he claimed, because his '41 Plymouth's first gear didn't work. So I only had to learn second and third gears and reverse, how to synchronize the clutch, brake, and gas pedals with shifting. "Without the first gear, it's going to be a little harder to get the car rolling forward smoothly, but you'll figure it out. Go on, get my keys out of my pants pocket. Now, don't wake up your folks, you know they wouldn't approve. You understand?"

I nodded.

"Take Extension Road to Baseline, then on to Transmission Road [now Gilbert] and straight to the farm. Do not go near town, you don't want to run into any cops. Now go!"

The car was parked parallel to the front yard. I looked around to make sure no one was watching, and then climbed into the front seat. I scooched the seat closer to the wheel, adjusted the rearview mirror, turned the key in the ignition, and pressed the starter button. (I didn't put on a seat belt, because seat belts hadn't been invented yet.) Placing my hand on the stick shift, I tested the gas pedal with my foot. Grandpa was right: it *was* similar to a tractor. Maybe this wouldn't be so difficult after all.

With great concentration, I shifted into second gear and gave it a little extra gas as instructed. The car lunged forward, bucking three times before the engine died. OK, maybe it wasn't going to be that easy. I tried it again with the same results. Third time was the charm, with just a little jerk. Was I ever grateful that none of my friends were there to see me. The car complained as I shifted to third gear, but it didn't die.

At the first stop, I only had to try twice to get a smooth start. By the time I'd driven the six miles to the farm I felt like a pro. I parked with a bit of a jolt, then got out, a swagger in my step. Lawrence and Andrew were milking and, as I'd predicted, had everything under control. Lola was helping. "Where's your grandpa?" she asked. After I explained the situation, she handed me her bucket without a word and headed to the house to make breakfast.

Grandpa's back problems lasted for three more days. Which gave me six more solitary commutes to and from the farm. Eventually my mom found out, but somehow he convinced her that it was all right. Anyway, she probably didn't want to get up at four thirty in the morning to take me.

Once Grandpa was up and moving, he was happy to let me drive morning and evening so he could relax in the passenger seat. We didn't tell Mom.

A couple of weeks later, I asked Grandpa if I could take the car to go to the movies. Apparently satisfied with the progress of my driving skills, he handed me the keys. Neither of us said a word to my folks as I headed out the door.

I picked up three buddies and then four girls and drove to the movies. To this day, I've never understood why any parent in their right mind would allow their kids to get in the car with a twelve-year-old driver. I sure wouldn't. The only thing I've been able to come up with is that they must have assumed an adult was driving the car. Wouldn't you?

The show was a double feature, including cartoons and reviews. At some point during the three or four hours we were at the movies, Mom must have put two and two together, and she had plenty of time to let her imagination run wild. Later, my parents would tell and retell this story time and again. Here's what they were doing while I was out having fun, not thinking a thing about it.

Mom paced the kitchen floor; Dad sat at the table with a cup of milk. "Howard," Mom said, "you should have stopped Herbie from taking Dad's car. He's been gone half the night. I know he's driven the car into a ditch. Maybe he drove into a canal and drowned! Go call the police, see if they've found him."

"Calm down, woman! The last thing we want to do is call the police. We'd all end up in jail. Anyway, how do you think I could have stopped him?"

"You must have heard the car start! It's all your fault, you should have never let him drive off."

"Think, Louise. Even if I had heard the car start, I wouldn't have thought that *your* dad was crazy enough to let our twelve-year-old son take his car. When it's dark, no less!"

"You know Dad lets him drive his car."

"Not at night. If you can just calm down, I'll go drive around and see if I can find him."

Dad had a hunch that I might be at the movies. He headed down Main Street to MacDonald, took a right, then another right onto First Street. There it was, the light-blue '41 Plymouth, parked in front of the Nile Theater.

Dad parked, and then asked the ticket-taker if he could check to see if I was there. Inside, the usher told him that there was a group of young kids near the front of the theater. Dad waited for his eyes to adjust to the dark, then spotted us, happily watching the movie and munching popcorn and licorice. Without letting us know he was there, he quietly left the theater and headed home to assure Mom that I wasn't floating facedown in the canal but at the theater with seven other kids.

When the screen finally went blank, my friends and I walked out and got in the car for the drive to seven homes scattered across Mesa proper and farther out into the farmlands. Dropping off everyone must have taken more than an hour, and when I finally did get home, the lights were on, and I knew I was in trouble. One foot in the door and Mom's *Reader's Digest* came flying through the air, hitting me square in the chest.

"Herbie!" Mom yelled. "Is your head screwed on right? What were you thinking?"

Somehow Dad got her calmed down. "It's late," he finally said, yawning. "Let's sleep on it. We'll take care of it tomorrow. Now go on, get to bed."

I escaped whatever might have happened "tomorrow" by being gone milking cows by the time they got up. I spent the day working on Grandpa's house with my uncles and Lola's sons, then did the evening milking before going home. During supper, the atmosphere was heavy, but my adventures of the night before were never brought up.

I think my driving episode was put to rest because Dad didn't see any real harm in what I had done, and he recognized the utility of my knowing how to drive. He could also tell that I had learned my lesson and that I wouldn't be joyriding again anytime soon. And maybe there was just a touch of admiration for my chutzpah, too.

CHICKEN SOUP

While writing this book, I've come to see how much my childhood revolved around cottonwood trees. One of my fondest memories is of my grandma sitting in the shade of a cottonwood tree, knitting and watching her kids play on the swing. I loved to climb cottonwoods, and swing from cottonwoods, and attempt to build tree houses in cottonwoods, and sneak off to meet girls using cottonwoods, and occasionally fall out of cottonwoods. Here is another cottonwood story, this time featuring some chickens.

A giant cottonwood tree grew on the bank of the eight-foot wide irrigation ditch across from my buddy Arnold's family's chicken pen. The tree's largest limb extended over the ditch, providing shade for the chicken run. Of course, such a branch was begging for three twelve-year-old boys—Arnold, Lee, and me—to tie a rope around it and experiment with swinging across the ditch, over the chicken run fence, and above the chicken coop, where we'd let go of the rope and land on the coop's roof.

Even though Lee and I were infinitely fascinated with the forces of physics, we just couldn't seem to find the solution to one minor problem: none of us had a clue as to where to tie the rope. Like the future scientists we were planning to be, we began to experiment using the well-worn method of trial and error.

The first test resulted in Arnold hitting the fence, losing his grip, and taking a bath with his clothes on in the irrigation ditch. This meant the rope was too long, so we shortened it. In the second test, Lee cleared the fence but was left dangling over a dozen Rhode Island Red layers and twice as many fryers pecking and clucking in the chicken run. This told us that the length of the rope was OK but not its location. I volunteered for test number three and slowly climbed out onto the limb and moved the rope a couple of feet closer to the chicken coop. I shimmied back to the trunk, and then climbed up a couple of feet to the next branch, which was perpendicular to the limb over the chicken run. I had covered all my bases: the pivot point was closer to the target, and I was farther from it and higher up so I'd get more velocity. The fence might prove a challenge; I would have to hold my legs up to clear it.

I tightened my grip on the rope and took a deep breath. The chickens continued their squabbling, unconcerned about the three boys nearby. With an exhale, I launched myself, swinging over the ditch, lifting my legs to perfectly avoid the fence. I'd made it! I was clear!

That's when it happened. The rope got tangled in a side branch, which caused it to jerk suddenly. I lost my grip and, with my legs still up high, I kept on flying, now untethered. Then gravity kicked in and I headed for the ground, butt first. To my great fortune—and her great misfortune—a Rhode Island Red hen broke my fall.

Arnold's family had a big pot of chicken soup for dinner. Needless to say, that was the end to our little rope-swing chicken-coop experiment.

EARTHQUAKES, FLYING PRINCIPALS, AND OTHER DISTRACTIONS

I'm not proud of the way I initially treated my eighth-grade teacher. (I don't remember her name, so I will call her Mrs. Wilson.) Mrs. Wilson must take part of the blame for her mistreatment, however, because she made the mistake of telling the class why she'd moved to Arizona from California: to get away from earthquakes.

California is situated on a few key faults that every so often give Mendocino or San Francisco or Long Beach a shake. There'd been an earthquake in El Centro in 1940 that registered 6.9 on the Richter scale, and apparently Mrs. Wilson had developed a serious phobia—so serious, in fact, that she uprooted her life and moved east. (I guess she was more afraid of the earth shaking than a scorpion crawling on her back in the middle of the night.)

Soon enough, I'd discovered that I could place the balls of my feet on the floor and, by bouncing my heels up and down, set it shaking and freak her out. Every so often, when I wanted to get out of taking a test or turning in an assignment or for the simple reason that I was bored, I would bounce the floor and watch her to see when my little prank had had its effect. Mrs. Wilson would freeze, the blood would drain from her face, and finally she'd scream, "Get outside! Get outside! We're having an earthquake!"

I'm sorry to admit that this was not my only method of distraction. As our homeroom teacher, Mrs. Wilson taught us all subjects, though her expertise was in math. (She was really a high school math teacher, but she'd been sent to our class because she was pregnant and the powers that be thought it would be easier for her to teach younger students—little did they know.) Whenever it was time to start English, a subject I had little interest in, I would ask her a random math question and thereby instigate a tangent that delayed any discussion of nouns and verbs. Later, I'd regret this, especially when I got to college and the admissions person told me, "Your scores are high, except in English. I should put you in dumbbell English." (People weren't as worried about political correctness or desk-side manner as they are today.)

Once, when Mrs. Wilson left to go to the bathroom (as she often did because she was pregnant), my friend Denzel Arrington and I took the pins out of the door hinges, then made a big ruckus so that the principal would hear us and come running. Which he did, and when he tried to make a grand entrance, the door went flying. Everyone started laughing, tears running down our faces as the principal, beet red, demanded to know who was the culprit. Not one of my classmates ratted me and Denzel out.

AN AGREEMENT IS AN AGREEMENT

That year, I got a job as a "pack-out boy" at the local grocery store. After school, I eagerly showed up for those first two weeks of work, bagging customers' groceries with a smile on my face, helping each customer—not just pregnant women or overburdened parents or the infirm—carry their bags out to their cars. I was excited to make a little cash, but I wasn't prepared for just how little cash I would make.

At the end of the pay period, my boss would just open the register and hand out our earnings without ceremony. My jaw dropped when I counted my cash, and I did a quick calculation in my head. I had been making 12.5¢ per hour. That's about $1.74 in today's money—way, way below minimum wage.

I was not a happy camper. When I got home, I told Grandpa about it. "Can you believe that?" I complained. "Twelve and a half cents per hour!"

Grandpa did not seem to share my outrage. "When you take a job," he said, "you make agreements. First, you agree to do the work. Your word is a promise, so you do the work you agree to do. Second, you agree on a salary. If you're dumb enough to work without that agreement, then you get whatever they give you."

This was not exactly the sympathetic response I'd been hoping for. But it did teach me a valuable lesson. After quitting that low-paying grocery job, from then on I always asked for the details before making an agreement.

BOYS DON'T COOK

I grew up at a time in which there were distinct roles for boys and girls, men and women. Back then, in my town, boys took a course that included drafting, woodworking, metal shop, and electrical and plumbing repair—every mom in Mesa had a pig-shaped cutting board—and girls took home economics, or "home ec," where they would learn how to sew and cook and manage a household budget in preparation for the housewives they were supposed to become.

I wanted to take the cooking classes, but the school wouldn't let me. I viewed cooking as chemistry, and if you do it right, the results of your experiment taste good. But I was told over and over again, "Boys don't cook!"

Later in the year, the home ec class cooked the shop class a big dinner. While the girls had learned how to set a formal table, we'd learned which of the utensils to use for which courses, a lesson I was grateful for because at home we just grabbed spoons and knives as needed out of the mason jars in the center of the table. Who knew there were different forks for salad versus the entrée? Who knew you weren't supposed to slurp your soup?

They sat us alternating boy, girl, boy, girl, with the boys standing to pull out the girls' chairs for them. (We'd also studied other important details of etiquette, like how to make polite small talk and how to ask a girl to a dance and then, once at the formal, how to dance.) I don't remember who sat on either side of me, but I do recall feeling jealous when they brought out the meal. I could do that, if only they'd let me!

A few decades later, I usually did the cooking whenever Gloria and I had friends over (as well as seven-course meals with wine pairings auctioned off at fund-raisers). I was the one to bring a sewing machine to the marriage, not her. I'd bought it for the manly reason of reupholstering my truck, but I'd also been inspired to take a night class on tailoring. I made myself a sports coat, and later I sewed costumes for the theater.

One evening, Gloria came in, dropped her sports equipment, took off her dirty shoes, and plopped down on the floor in the hallway with her back leaning against the wall. "I'm so tired," she said, then took one look at me in the dining room and started laughing. There I was, sewing away, while she'd been out playing tackle football. So much for gender roles.

UNINVITED TO THE CANTATA

We were preparing a musical adaptation of the story of Rip van Winkle for the All Eighth-Grade Cantata. The music teacher was adamant about us humming *nnnnn* instead of the classic *mmmmm* because it was, according to her, "cleaner and crisper." It proved to be a hard habit to break, and out of complete frustration, our five-foot-four-inch, two-hundred-plus-pound teacher decided to take drastic measures. To really get our attention and make it count, she hummed *nnnnn* at the top of her lungs while simultaneously running across the room and jumping up on the piano bench with both feet. I'm not sure what she was expecting, but presumably it wasn't all four legs of the bench collapsing out from under her. Her hum-yelling *nnnnn* took on a higher pitch as she fell, landing spread-eagle on the floor with a thud. For a moment there was silence.

A few of us seemed to find this scene funny, and once she recovered, we got a lecture on how it's impolite to laugh at someone who's had an accident. Though maybe it didn't go exactly as planned, her little demonstration worked. Never again was *mmmmm* heard in her classroom.

The day before the cantata was to be performed in the high school theater, the music teacher took me aside and said, "I'm sorry, Herb, but the bleachers onstage only hold two hundred seventy-five students. We have two hundred seventy-eight students in the choir, including more basses than needed . . ." I must have looked confused, because she continued. "I am asking you to sit out of the musical."

I was far from heartbroken, but still I found it strange. Forty-four years later, at a class reunion, I found out that my buddy Denzel, a baritone, had been told that there were too many *baritones* in the musical. We never found out who the third uninvited student was, nor whether it was our inability to sing or revenge on for us laughing so hard that caused us to be barred from the performance. Whatever the reason, it took a toll on me. To this day, I won't sing in public, even "Happy Birthday" at a party. I do, however, sing in the shower.

DON'T FALL ASLEEP IN CHURCH

In the Mormon Church, the service usually opens with the congregation singing a hymn, followed by a member being called upon to give the opening prayer. After the emblems of the sacrament are blessed and passed around, a member gives a prepared sermon, and a final hymn is sung, another member gives the closing prayer.

For an older man named Brother Dees, the opening hymn was like a lullaby. (Though his first name was Preston, I never heard him called anything but Brother Dees.) He was something of a self-appointed patriarch of the ward who also seemed to be perpetually sleepy. One evening, he happened to be sitting next to me, and he was down for the count by the end of the opening hymn's second verse.

As the hymn concluded and the congregation fell silent, I gave Brother Dees a little nudge. He opened his eyes and blinked. "Psst," I whispered. "The bishop called on you to give the closing prayer."

He nodded once and stood up, then walked directly to the pulpit and closed the meeting. A ripple of confusion went through the church. The bishop stood up and approached the pulpit. Looking me straight in the eye, he said, "Herb Bryce, come up here and apologize to Brother Dees, then reopen the meeting with a prayer."

I don't think Brother Dees ever sat next to me or talked to me again. He also never again fell asleep in church.

THINGS GO BOOM

That spring, I was helping Grandpa remove some trees on the farm by using dynamite to break up the tree's root ball and taproot. Grandpa made some big errors in judgment that day. First, he told me where he kept the key to the wooden chest in which the dynamite was stored. Second, he showed me how to put the fuse, blasting cap, and dynamite together. Third, he showed me how to place the dynamite under the root ball in order to maximize the blast. Fourth, he let me place the dynamite and light the fuse.

After dynamiting three trees, I thought I was a dynamite expert. For a few weeks, I kept my guardian angels on their toes. What kind of damage would half a stick of dynamite cause to a watermelon? There was only one way to find out. Can a fuse burn underwater? I discovered that indeed it could. What would happen if someone were to light half a stick of dynamite and throw it into deep water? You get a big spout of water and a few stunned fish floating to the surface.

I wish that I could say that I put a halt to my experiments because it dawned on me that what I was doing was stupid and dangerous. But, as you might have figured out by now, that's not really how my mind worked. The real reason I stopped fooling around with dynamite was because I was afraid Grandpa would notice that his supply was dwindling.

A few weeks later, Lawrence was looking around the shed for some parts to fix the hay baler when he discovered crystals in a slit between the boards of the dynamite chest. He opened the chest to find crystals not just in the corner but also at the bottom of one of the boxes of dynamite. The presence of those crystals meant that the nitroglycerin had been seeping out of the absorbent, making it extremely dangerous. Thank goodness that I wasn't taking dynamite out of that particular box.

Lawrence, Andrew, and I decided to very gingerly carry the entire chest way out into the field and bring in all of the livestock and fence them at a safe distance in the corral. While Lawrence got his hunting rifle, I placed a box of dynamite on top of the wooden chest, then put a box of blasting caps on top of that.

We ran to the edge of the field, and Lawrence handed me the rifle. I took four shots before getting a hit.

The sixty pounds of dynamite created the loudest blast I have ever heard in my life. It shattered some windows in Grandpa's house, and the nearest neighbor, at about a hundred yards away, claimed it had broken two of his windows. That blast was a great lesson in humility; it made me realize that dynamite deserved much more respect than I'd been giving it. We spent the weekend filling in the crater it made and leveling the field.

Though I'd been humbled, I wasn't cured of my love of making things go boom. Soon after the dynamite drama, I discovered a large can of carbide (calcium carbide) in the shed. Grandpa often used a "miner's lamp," which, through combining water and carbide, forms acetylene, a highly flammable gas. After letting the pressure of the reaction build up, you open the valve on top of the lamp and ignite the gas to get a flame that's much brighter than a kerosene lamp, making it a good light for irrigating at night.

Imagine the possibilities this magical substance has for a kid. Instead of igniting the gas, put a cork in the neck of the bottle and let the pressure build up—and now you have a popgun. Take your finger off the cork and POW! There goes the cork. Another pre-paintball game. (If my grandkids are reading this: Forget it. Glass bottles have been known to shatter if the cork is too tight. Do as I say and not as I did! There's a reason I waited until you grew up before writing this book—for your safety.)

Further rummaging around in the shed provided a foot-long scrap of two-and-a-half-inch galvanized pipe that must have been cut from a longer length, because it had threads on one end and a burred cut-off on the other. We found a cap that fit the pipe in an old wooden apple crate, and, with a grinder, we rounded off the burrs, then filed the inside edge smooth. Then we bored an eighth-of-an-inch hole just above the cap.

Pour in a little water, add three or four pellets of carbide, wait a few seconds, plug the end tightly with a wad of newspaper, then bring a flame up to the hole, and BOOOOM! We'd just made ourselves a cannon.

One big problem: the wad of newspaper caught fire. I remembered that flaming arrow setting the grass on fire in Goodyear, and I didn't want that to happen again. (See, sometimes I do learn my lesson.) What could we substitute for the newspaper?

Grandpa's dog loved to play fetch with an old tennis ball, which would be the perfect size. I ran and got it, thankful that the dog wasn't there to get his hopes up, and dipped it in the cows' watering trough so that it would be wet and therefore not become a fireball. This time we experimented with letting the acetylene gas and air mix before plugging the end with the tennis ball, the idea being that this would give us the biggest explosion.

We aimed it at the outhouse and missed, the ball flying way over the roof and out into the alfalfa field. A long search brought us up empty-handed. What could we substitute for the tennis ball?

Arnold and I came up with the bright idea of using an old rusty ten-gallon milk can. Add about a quart of water, drop in a handful of carbide, pound the lid on with a rubber mallet, and stand *way* back.

We set the can on a mound of dry cow manure, ran to the edge of the field, and waited and waited and waited. No explosion came. After thirty seconds or so, Arnold began to walk slowly toward the can.

"Get back here," I yelled. "It could explode any second and the lid could hit you!"

"No," he yelled back. "I hear a hissing sound. The milk can has a hole in it! I gotta find it."

Arnold took a Zippo lighter out of his pocket, lit it, and ran the flame down the rusty seam of the can . . .

BOOM!!!

The lid went flying straight up in the air, at least seventy-five feet high. Arnold fell backward and rolled down the manure mound. The lid landed on the other side of the mound; the milk can split along its seam. Fortunately, he was unscathed (he must have had a group of guardian angels protecting him, too), but he was covered head to toe in dry cow manure. I laughed my head off for at least five minutes.

That episode with the carbide finally scared some sense into us. I stopped playing with things that go boom, at least for a little while. Later, as a teacher, for in-class demonstrations, I used our crude pipe design to make a cannon out of three-inch PVC plastic pipe. A four-inch Nerf ball was its fodder, perfect because you can squeeze the spongy foam plastic down to fit the pipe and dampen it with water to make it fireproof. Plus Nerf balls come in bright colors, making them easy to see as they fly overhead. They might not travel as fast as a tennis ball or be as theatrical as a rusty milk can, but you won't get hurt if you get hit with it. You're less likely to end up covered in cow shit, too.

GRANDPA REMARRIES . . . AGAIN

I'd bet my every last cent that Grandpa married wife number four purely out of spite. Though he and Lola were able to get along well enough to keep the farm running, he was clearly still bent out of shape over her contact with her ex. Grandpa never could be without a woman, so not only would a new relationship get Lola's goat, it would provide him with that female companionship he needed.

North of the Grand Canyon, there was a polygamist town called Short Creek (renamed Colorado City in 1960). Every few years, Arizona's governor would want to make a political point about polygamy and initiate a raid. Big clouds of dust would signal to the townspeople that trouble was on its way, and by the time the police arrived, the men would be gone and the women would be standing outside singing hymns. Still, all wives besides the first were not recognized as legal by the state, and so they would have to go elsewhere to avoid charges of bigamy or polygamy. For some, like young girls who'd been forced into marriage or those whose husbands were abusive, these raids were a blessing. But for those who were content with their lot as second or third or fourth wives, this was less a disaster than a headache—often the women would leave town, only to come back once the dust had settled.

Eva Spenser belonged to the latter group. A raid on Short Creek had her at loose ends, and she arrived in time to take up residence with Grandpa in his new house on the property he shared with Lola. It's unclear whether she and Grandpa got married, or even whether he and Lola had officially gotten divorced. I do know that, at some point, the church called him in for a lecture and a threat of excommunication. This might have been because of the dubious status of his various relationships, or it could have been because he'd taken to "helping Lola irrigate" at night, leaving his new bride behind to meet his ex in the field, where they claimed he helped her with the crops.

Eva didn't seem to mind the situation—she'd come from a polygamist marriage, after all—but the church did. The problem was solved six months later, when the governor moved on from Short Creek and it was safe for her to return. Grandpa and Lola remarried or, if they had never actually divorced, moved back in together in 1950. They'd be together for the remainder of his life.

CHAPTER 8

High School, Here I Come: 1947–1949

The hay had been baled, hauled in, and stacked. My uncle Talmage, Lola's boys Lawrence and Andrew, and I were sitting around on bales of alfalfa after a hard day's work. I'd managed to finish eighth grade without blowing myself up or getting expelled, what I would call a successful year. Now it was summer, the season of infinite possibilities for making trouble. I was thirteen years old.

Our first grand idea was to load up the pickup with inner tubes and head out to the Eastern Canal, a major canal with an eight-foot wide maintenance road running parallel to it. We inflated four inner tubes, patching one that had developed a hole over the past school year, and tossed them in the back of the truck. Talmage and I followed Lawrence and Andrew in my uncle's car. We parked downstream, where it would be easy to exit the canal, then jumped in the back of the pickup and headed upstream a couple miles.

Once in the canal, I dragged my hands and feet in the cold water as we leisurely floated along. To this day, I've never found a better way to cool off on a hot day than an inner tube ride in a lazy current. I completely relaxed, the tedium of schoolwork and the effort of baling hay a distant memory. Then someone mentioned finding a boat with an outboard motor to pull us up and down the canal. Floating was all well and good, but being pulled—that was exciting!

We continued to discuss the subject during milking that evening. No one could think of anyone who had a motorboat. Then it hit me. "Why don't we just tie the inner tube to the bumper of a car?" I said.

"You can't steer inner tubes, dummy," Talmage said. "The rope would just pull them out of the canal and up onto the road."

Though my idea had been quashed, we weren't done with the topic. The next day after milking and breakfast, Talmage came up with a great idea. "Why don't we make a surfboard, tie it to the bumper, and ride it up and down the canal?"

Seemed like a good idea to me. We searched the lumber scrap pile but could not come up with a one-inch-thick board that would be wide enough to stand on. Lawrence said he knew where he might be able to find something. He ran into the house and came out with his mom's ironing board. "Mom has been griping about getting a new ironing board. We get a surfboard, she gets a new ironing board. Kill two birds with one stone."

After removing the cover, legs, and hardware, rounding both ends and smoothing them with sandpaper, and installing a rope handle and an eyebolt—voilà!—we had our one-inch-thick, sixteen-inch-wide, five-foot-long surfboard. I ran to the shed and came back with a fifty-foot half-inch rope. We were ready to head to the canal and try it out.

We enlisted Maxine, who was afraid to swim in deep water but didn't mind driving. The bumper was not high enough to keep the rope from dragging along the bank of the canal, so we tied the rope to the car's doorpost and set the makeshift surfboard in the water. Since this had been Talmage's idea, he got to take the maiden voyage.

He got in the canal and stood on the board in the water, then picked up the rope handle. The rest of us got into the car, Maxine behind the wheel. "OK!" Talmage shouted. "Let's go!"

Maxine turned the key in the ignition and slowly eased forward. I looked out the back window. The board seemed to be sinking underneath Talmage. "You're going to have to go faster than that," I said. Encouraged, she put the pedal to the medal, and soon we were cruising at thirty miles an hour, the wind blowing through the open car windows.

"Yahoo!" Talmage shouted before getting tossed into the canal with a big splash. Each of us took a turn, with only one minor injury occurring that summer. Well, Andrew might not have considered getting thrown and his face hitting the muddy bottom of the canal minor, but it was to me.

We did have to pitch in and buy Lola a new ironing board. It was worth it.

I COULD HAVE GONE ALL DAY WITHOUT THAT

For those cows who tended to kick, we used hobbles, a simple contraction with two cuffs linked together and placed on the hind legs above the hocks. (Back then, it was made of steel; today, dairy farmers usually use ones made of durable nylon or propylene. You'll soon see why.) This was mostly to prevent a cow from putting her foot into the milk bucket or kicking the bucket over.

One summer evening I was milking Molly, a cow with a reputation for kicking. There were a lot of flies buzzing around, an annoyance common around the cow pies the cows regularly deposited. They were landing on Molly's flank, and she was not very happy about it, giving a full-body shiver every now and then and swishing her tail back and forth to drive them off. The trouble was that when she swung her tail to the right, she'd give my head, which was inconveniently placed so that I could reach the udder, a swat. A slap upside the head with a cow's tail is not only a nuisance—it hurts.

To stop her from swatting me, I used the long hair at the end of her tail to tie it to the hobbles. Mission accomplished, I sat down on my one-legged stool, placed the bucket between my knees, and resumed milking. That seemed to solve the problem for a while, at least for me. But the flies hadn't given up on their buzzing, and the cow, unable to swish at them, instigated plan B.

The next thing I knew, she'd somehow managed to step out of the hobbles, and around came her tail with the steel hobbles still attached. BAM! The hobbles struck the side of my head, hitting me so hard that it knocked me over. The bucket, over three quarters full of milk, came with me.

The next thing I knew, I was lying on the concrete floor covered in warm milk. I looked up to see Grandpa, Lawrence, and Andrew not coming over to help me but instead sitting there, laughing their heads off. Meanwhile, the cow was still swishing her tail and its attached hobbles above me.

"Someone grab her tail so I can get up!" I yelled.

Andrew finally recovered enough from his hysterics to come to my rescue. The first thing I did once I was upright was to remove the hobbles from the cow's tail. After I took my stool off, Andrew grabbed the hose and sprayed me down, clothes and all. Dripping wet, I strapped the stool back on and finished milking the cow. With the weather being over 100 degrees with low humidity, I was dry, though sticky, by the time I finished milking the next cow. I learned my lesson—I never tied a cow's tail to the hobbles again.

TARGET PRACTICE

Since my seventh birthday, when I milked seven cows and nearly killed myself doing so, I had developed a very strong grip. I could squeeze a stream of milk in an approximately six-foot trajectory and with pretty good aim. If a fly landed on the edge of the bucket, one quick squirt and it was gone.

One of our rat-catchers—a.k.a. cats—that roamed the haystack looking for rodents would come in the corral and stand around waiting for one of us to shoot a stream of milk her way. We had trained her to stand on her back legs and catch the milk in her mouth by squirting the stream higher and higher. Eventually she was able to stand completely upright on her hind feet.

Meanwhile, Lola had trained us to come to her house after working in the field and before afternoon milking, for a snack to hold us over until supper. My favorite snack was a quart of milk and half a fruit pie, warmed in the oven. As Dad would say, "I only like two kinds of pie: hot and cold."

BUILDING A HOUSE

One day when I was sitting at the table writing in my note-book, Dad approached and asked me if he could have a sheet of notepaper. He ripped it out of my three-ring binder, sat down at the table, and with a pencil and ruler, drew a schematic of a three-bedroom, one-bath house. This he took to the bank and, based on that rudimentary sketch, got a loan.

A week later, we were pouring the footings and foundation on the property Dad had purchased from Jearl's brother Bud. The following week we poured the concrete floors, dyed a deep red, what they call today "oxblood." We used concrete blocks for the exterior and interior walls, and concrete red roofing tiles for the roof. Plaster was applied to the interior walls to make them smooth.

My dad, my uncles, and I built the entire thing, from floor to ceiling to roof. Dad was in charge, and I was the grunt, per usual. My job was to keep Dad, Jearl, and Talmage supplied with concrete blocks and mortar. When all the blocks were laid, we plastered over the entire interior and applied a finish coat. Guess who mixed the plaster? You're right, it was me.

Dad paid me a little spending money, enough for a couple of movie tickets and a popcorn, plus a sundae on the way home. More than the pocket change, it was about the apprenticeship, which allowed me to get a good-paying summer job with a masonry contractor the next summer, before I moved to Fontana, California, to start my sophomore year.

Before plastering, we did the electric wiring and plumbing. This was before copper pipes; we used galvanized iron pipes, which I cut and threaded before my uncles installed them. When they started on the cabinets, I was assigned to dig the cesspool. There was no sewer system yet, and the ground had a clay layer about three or four feet below the surface, so we could not have a simple drain field. Therefore, we had to build a cesspool system that required digging a hole about four feet in diameter under the clay layer, in a section made of sand, gravel, and rock. This ended up being about fifteen feet below ground. How did we get that fifteen-foot hole? With a pick and shovel. When the hole was too deep to throw the dirt out, we used a winch and a five-gallon bucket to hoist it up to surface level. To get into or out of the hole, we stood in the bucket used to lower the concrete blocks and mortar with one foot and held on to the rope while someone above cranked the winch.

Here is an example of a well wench. Ours was homemade and looked crude compared to this one.

We put down a layer of concrete blocks on their side so the holes were exposed, as a reinforcement wall to prevent the walls from collapsing. The holes in the blocks were open in the sand, gravel, and rock section for drainage, and laid so that the wall was solid above that. We built the septic tank in the top four feet, leaving space above for a layer of dirt. I got to practice laying blocks during the lining of the cesspool and septic tank. No one would ever see the glory of my artistic endeavor—or my boo-boos—once the lid was in place.

DATING OFFICIALLY BEGINS

The house was finished a month before school started. To earn some money during the school year, I got a job as box boy at Wright's Super Market; I was shortly promoted to restock boy and backup box boy. On Saturdays, I worked in the morning, leaving my afternoons free. That funded my "Wanna go . . . ?" non-date dates and gave me time to spend my money. When the swimming pool closed for the winter, I invited Helen and Ann skating or to the Friday-night dances at the Mezona, a giant dance hall purchased by the Mormon Church in 1926, in a noncommittal way by saying, "Dad's taking me to the Mezona. Wanna come along?"

The word "date" entered my vocabulary when it came to school dances and girls other than Helen and Ann. Mesa High had three formal dances: the Freshman–Sophomore Hop (at least one of the couple had to be a freshman or soph-omore), the Co-Ed (girls ask boys, open to all grades), and the Junior–Senior Prom (at least one of the couple had to be a junior or senior). The Mormon Church had three formal dances: Harvest Ball, Christmas Formal, and the Gold and

Green Ball. The age limits for these dances were high school student through great-grandparent. My freshman year, I attended all but the Junior–Senior Prom.

All the formals were intended for dancing, with a live big band orchestra and lots of crepe paper decorations in the spacious auditorium. Boys and men wore suits and ties. (On rare occasions, someone would show up in a tuxedo.) Girls and women wore floor-length evening gowns. When making the date, I would ask the color of the lucky gal's gown so that I could choose a corsage that would complement her dress and the color of her hair. She, in turn, would give me a boutonniere.

At the entrance, female chaperones stood with a big box of fine netting in every color of the rainbow, so they could create a matching cover over any strapless dress or evening gown that was deemed too low cut. I surmise that they did not really think this over, given that driving alone to and from the dance in the privacy of a car afforded ample opportunity to get up to monkey business, certainly a more appealing option than on the dance floor with a hundred other couples. Some of the girls wore the netting as a badge of defiance.

The dances always started with a grand march, after which there was a pause so boys could reserve dances with the girls, everyone filling out their dance card for the evening.

For the high school formal dances, if one person in the couple was old enough to drive, then a dinner at an upscale restaurant or a nightclub was part of the evening. This meant they had to find one that was open until 2:00 a.m. for after the dance, necessitating a drive to Phoenix, about fifteen miles west of Mesa.

You'll notice that work, dating, and surfboard fun take primary place in my memories of that time, which might seem incongruous given that I was to become a teacher and spend almost the entirety of my adult life inside the classroom. I think this can be explained by a combination of raging hormones, the desire for self-sufficiency and autonomy, and the fact that most of the time in school I was bored out of my mind. School was just school, a place to go and do enough schoolwork to get good grades. I would spend my career rectifying this situation—education is one of the most important things in the world, and I would do my best to make sure that my classes were exciting enough to take a larger place in my students' memory.

HI-HO, HI-HO

As freshman year wound down, I began looking for a full-time job for the summer. Mike, a masonry contractor, and my uncle Jearl were neighbors. One day they were talking, and Mike mentioned that he was looking for a hod carrier, and Jearl recommended me. Mike called me up and said the job was mine if I wanted it—and that he'd pay me $1.75 an hour, just 25 cents less than bricklayers, and a princely sum for a teenager. I couldn't believe it! I jumped at the offer before he could change his mind.

Because of the summer heat in Arizona, our working hours were 5:00 a.m. to 2:30 p.m. It was a great schedule because it gave me time off in the afternoons and early evenings. I rode in to work with Mike a little early so that we could get ready for the bricklayers. He'd start the cement mixer and we'd have a batch of mortar prepped by the time the bricklayers arrived. While the mixer was running, I would make sure that each bricklayer would have a stack of bricks waiting for them as soon as they got there.

A man with a brick hod. I used one of these on the job to carry bricks and mortar for the brick layers!

As a hod carrier, my main job was to haul those bricks to wherever they were needed. If the walls were shorter than six feet, I would use the wheelbarrow. Above that height, I would switch to the official tool: the brick hod. A brick hod is a V-shaped, three-sided box for holding up to twelve bricks and mortar, with a long handle so you can carry it over the shoulder. It was designed so that you can climb a ladder with it, too. As you can imagine, this was sweaty, exhausting work.

On the way home one day, Mike got around to asking me how old I was.

"Fourteen," I said.

"What?" he said. "If I had known that, I would never have offered you the job." He paused, and for a second I was afraid he was going to fire me. After a moment, he continued, "I am glad I didn't know. The guy you replaced was more than twice your age, but you can work circles around him. Jearl said you were a hard worker, and boy was that an understatement. Makes me tired just watching you."

"When I helped Jearl and my dad build their houses," I said, "we used concrete blocks, and I mixed the mortar in a mortar tub with a hoe. Bricks and a cement mixer make the job a whole lot easier."

Mike laughed. "You're probably the first person who's told me that hod carrying was easier than, well, anything. You've got a job as long as you want one." I didn't say anything. He sighed. "I guess I'll be losing you when school starts in September."

WATCH WHERE YOU SPRAY THAT PAINT

Mike the masonry contractor was right. My aunt Maxine had graduated from high school that past May of 1948, and Talmage had graduated from Arizona State College in June. He'd accepted a position teaching fifth grade in the Fontana School District, in San Bernardino County, California. He called my dad and told him that Kaiser Steel, located in Fontana, was looking for welders. The pay was much better than Reynold's Aluminum, where Dad had been working, so Dad applied and got the job.

And so it was time to move again. Since Maxine was living with us, it made sense that she would go with the family. I moved in with Falene and Jearl so that I could continue to work that summer while my parents packed.

My masonry job ended the first week of August, when the bricklayers completed the second house. Jearl was completing a duplex, and he talked me into staying and helping him dig a cesspool. It was an easy sell, as this would be my third dig, and it was a lot cooler at the bottom of the hole than out in the hot sun. Most of all, I had never been to Fontana and had no idea what I would do there until school started, and I wasn't all that anxious to make the move.

Summer did eventually come to an end, and so I said goodbye to Helen and Ann, to Mike and Jearl and Falene, and went to live with my folks out west.

My uncle Callis had just graduated from chiropractic school and bought a three-story turn-of-the century house in Riverside, about ten or eleven miles from my folks. The bottom floor was his office, the second floor was their living quarters, and the third floor was a rental apartment. The house had potential but was in serious need of painting, and since I still had just over a couple of weeks before my sophomore year started, Callis offered me the job. I moved into their spare bedroom, which would become the nursery room four months later.

Callis was convinced that I could finish before school started, meaning I had sixteen days to paint ground to roof. Callis opened the door to the detached garage to show me the supplies: an eight-foot ladder and a thirty-six-foot extension ladder, twenty gallons of light-blue-gray paint, five gallons of dark-blue-gray paint, a wire brush, and one-inch and three-inch paintbrushes. Though the technology of paint rollers had been invented, they were not yet available in Southern California.

Callis scheduled appointments with his chiropractic clientele for only three days a week so he could help with the painting. By the end of the first week, we'd finished the front of the building and the wraparound porch. The unlikelihood of our completing the project before school started was becoming obvious.

"You could get it done with a paint spray gun over the Labor Day weekend," he said, then bought the spray gun and compressor the next day. I helped him move the extension ladder, and we took turns climbing up and administering a spray of paint. He was right about how fast the painting went, but one thing he hadn't considered was the collateral spray.

At the end of the day, we discovered that four of the cars parked on the street in front of the house were covered in tiny dots of paint. The lucky thing was that the paint spray floating through the air was already partially dry by the time it landed on the car roofs and windshields, making it easier to remove. On Labor Day, I added a few tasks to my to-do list: washing, removing all splatter using car polish, and waxing the neighbors' cars.

A LONELY BEGINNING TO SOPHOMORE YEAR

Chaffey High School, located in Ontario, California, served seven cities in western San Bernardino County. It shared the campus with the two-year Chaffey College, as well as some of the classrooms and faculty (a college professor taught my sophomore geometry class). The joint enrollment was well over five thousand students, a big increase from the smaller student population in Mesa. (The following year, Mesa would organize a huge parade in honor of the one thousandth student to enroll.) In the beginning, I didn't know a soul; it was easy to get lost in the crowded lunchroom and in the hustle and bustle of the hallways.

My sophomore year was pretty much a throwaway year for me—that is, until spring. I did make the football team, managing to break my thumb early in the season. I played with a cast, which the coach padded by taping on a quarter inch of foam rubber whenever I played. It should not have been allowed, both because it only slowed the healing process and because it essentially gave me a club at the end of my arm. The broken thumb did earn me an A in typing—an A for effort from the sympathetic teacher. And I surprised myself by winning first place in a mono-color painting contest, in which we could only use one color plus white to create lighter shades and black for darker shades. I chose to paint a turtle surfacing because of the squares on the shell, and the transparent water allowed the use of different shades of greenish-blue.

Chaffey was fourteen miles west of Fontana and nearly an hour's bus ride. Because sports practice took up the last period of the day plus an hour after school, to go home I took the late bus, which serviced Upland, Rancho Cucamonga, and Fontana, which was at the end of the route. This meant that I left home at 6:30 a.m. to walk to the bus stop and got home at about 6:00 p.m. These were long days, but at least I didn't have to get up at four thirty to milk the cows.

I didn't share a class with a single student on my bus, and because there were so many students from all over the area, it was hard for me to make close friends. Our church was very small and only had a total of three high school boys in the congregation, me and a set of twins who were seniors. They did not want to hang out with a lowly sophomore. There were also four high school girls: a freshman, whose parents said she was too young to date (or at least that's what she told me, though it could have been her way of avoiding me), two juniors who were dating the twins, and Cathy.

A DUD OF A DOUBLE DATE

Cathy was a senior and a double cousin of the twins—her mother was the sister of the twins' father, and her father was the brother of the twins' mother. Maxine had met her fiancé, Paul, at church; he was Cathy's brother. Cathy was very friendly at church, but in real life, she too wasn't all that keen about hanging out with someone two grades below her.

We were in a city now, and I could no longer get away with driving without a driver's license. We had one car, and Mom did not like to drive at night, so if I wanted to get any-where, I had to either walk, ride my bicycle, or convince Dad to give me a ride. Needless to say, my circle of friends started small and stayed small.

Maxine was living with us, and one night while Paul was visiting, I overheard the two of them talking about going to the movies. With zero nonchalance, I told them that I'd like to see the movie. "Do you think I could talk Cathy into going?" I asked.

"I'll talk to her," Paul offered.

This was a huge mistake! Paul was a former Marine ser-geant, and his version of "talk to her" translated to "You're going." Your future uncle-in-law issuing directives is not the best way to win over a girl, particularly if that man happens to be her big brother. Still, Cathy agreed, though I'm pretty sure she made it clear to Paul and Maxine how she felt about the situation.

That Friday, when Paul came to pick up Maxine, I jumped in the back seat. I'd assumed that we were going to pick up Cathy, but she drove herself and was waiting for us outside the theater. She gave me a half smile when I approached. Though she didn't seem all that excited to see me, she did let me buy her ticket.

At the concession stand, Paul said, "Herb, get you and Cathy a large bag of popcorn. I'll get one for Maxine and me." That was already my plan—I'd been well trained to be a gentleman by my dad and grandpa—but I just nodded.

Inside the theater, Maxine entered the row first, followed by Paul. I stepped aside to let Cathy enter, then followed her. As soon as we were settled in, Cathy stood up and announced that she was going to get her own bag of popcorn. *That's strange,* I thought to myself. "I have a bag for us to share," I said. She ignored me, squeezing past and quickly heading out the door to the lobby. She came back down the opposite aisle with a small bag of popcorn in hand and took a seat next to Maxine.

"Herb's on the other side," Maxine pointed out.

"I know, but I want to sit by you tonight," Cathy said. Talk about sending a message!

This non-date date did not end our friendship. I understood that she felt I was too young. The following Sunday she apologized and let me know that she still wanted to be my friend. "I was mad at Paul," she admitted, "and I took it out on you."

"I'm sorry, too," I said. "I should have asked you directly." Fortunately, I did not lose one of my few new friends—our friendship was made stronger by resolving this misunderstanding.

THE DANCE THAT ALMOST WASN'T

In the spring the church announced the date of the Stake Gold and Green Ball. This annual social event brought the teenagers of several wards together for some wholesome mingling.

After Sunday school that day, Cathy said that she wished she had somebody to go with.

"I can take you," I said without hesitation. "I love to dance."

"Sure you can," she said.

I took that as a yes. This was going to be my first date as a sophomore. I'd gone to the birthday party of a girl from study hall who lived in Upland, fifteen miles northwest of Fontana. Dad had grumbled all the way there and, at the end of the party when he had to pick me up, all the way back. That was the closest thing to a date up until now. So you can imagine how excited I was.

The day of the ball, I jumped on my bicycle and rode to the florist and picked up a corsage, a bloom of pink roses, the nicest one I could afford. The ball would be held in San Bernardino, about twelve miles east of Fontana, and I'd asked Paul and Maxine, who were married by then, if they wouldn't mind giving us a ride. Right on time, they picked me up and together we headed to Cathy's. "Go get 'er," Paul encouraged me as I got out of the car.

I stood on the front stoop in my suit and tie, holding Cathy's corsage proudly in hand. I took a deep breath, and then rang the doorbell. After a minute, the door opened and on the other side of the threshold there was Cathy, in a pull-over and shorts. Her hair was pulled back in a loose ponytail and her feet were bare. She didn't have a stitch of makeup on her very surprised face. "Oh my God," she said. "I thought you were joking."

For a moment I didn't say anything. Finally, I cleared my throat. "When you said, 'Sure you can,' I thought that was a yes."

"I'm so sorry, Herb. I was being sarcastic. I . . . uh . . . I know you're not old enough to drive, so I didn't take you seriously. I'm sorry."

I offered her the corsage.

"I can't take it," she said, her hands at her sides. "It's not fair to you."

"I should have asked instead of saying 'I can take you,'" I said. "It's my fault. You're my friend, and I bought it for you. I want you to have it."

She took the corsage, and I noticed she had tears in her eyes.

"I'll see you on Sunday," I said.

"Thank you," she said, closing the door. "See you Sunday."

Brokenhearted and thoroughly embarrassed, I turned and walked back to the car. *I am a total idiot,* I thought. I climbed in the back and slouched down in the seat. "Paul," I said, "will you take me home?"

"The hell I will," he said. "She's going to the dance!" Marine Sergeant Marshall got out of the car and marched up to the front door. Without knocking or ringing the door-bell, he opened it and entered the house, slamming the door behind him. I slouched down even further. We could hear shouting coming from inside. Then there was silence. Maxine turned around and looked at me, then turned back and rested her head on the window to wait. What felt like an eternity but was probably fifteen minutes passed.

Then the door opened and there stood, framed in the doorway, my year-long crush, wearing a blue evening gown, her hair combed and makeup applied, the corsage properly placed on her wrist. In her hand was a makeshift boutonniere that her mother had crafted from a rose she cut from the corsage while Cathy was getting dressed. My heart skipped a beat.

Paul opened the car door for his sister, and she slid in next to me. I sat up straight. Paul, still in sergeant mode, turned his head and, staring at Cathy, commanded, "Apologize to Herb!"

In an even louder voice, I shouted, "Leave her alone! You have humiliated her enough. It was my fault, not hers. If you want to yell at someone, yell at me!"

Paul shrugged and then started the car. About ten minutes into the drive, Cathy reached over and gently squeezed my hand. She mouthed the words "Thank you." I squeezed back. "You're welcome," I whispered. Then silence.

We pulled into the church's parking lot, and Paul found a spot under a lamppost. I got out and walked around to the other side so I could open Cathy's door. I took her hand and she stepped into the light. Without thinking, I blurted, "Wow! You look stunning." She gave me a big smile. We were on the road to recovery.

As we were dancing, she tried once more to apologize. I responded, "Hey, that's all behind us. Let's just have fun and enjoy tonight." After a pause, I added, "I wish I were older right now."

"Are you sure you're *not* eighteen?" she asked. After that remark, I knew the evening was going to turn out OK.

We held hands on the way home, and a good-night kiss on the cheek made the whole affair worth it. A couple of weeks later, Cathy called and asked if I would like to go to the movies with her. "I'll pick you up at six thirty," she said, "and I'm buying the popcorn." My sophomore year was finally looking up.

CHAPTER 9

My Last Years of Childhood: 1949–1950

My maternal grandparents' oldest daughter, Irene, had married Milton Roe, a man fourteen years her senior, in 1923, when she was only seventeen. They were a strange couple. She was a head taller than he was and, having lived in the Deep South for her childhood, she wholly embraced the part of the Southern belle. Milton, on the other hand, was a loner with the physique of a twelve-year-old and an unending series of get-rich-quick schemes. While he was off trying to get his current venture off the ground, Irene worked as a waitress at the most expensive restaurant in Arizona to pay the rent and keep food on the table.

The summer after my sophomore year, Milton was prospecting for copper, molybdenum, manganese, and silver, staking out claims and then selling them for a profit. He invited me to go along with him and his son, Junior, to the drop-off point at the base of the mountain. We drove as far up into the mountains as the federal roads would take us. At the end of the road, we unloaded the mules, strapped on the panniers, and loaded them up with a month's worth of supplies. Milton told his son a date to return and pick him and the mules up. With that, he took off his well-worn Stetson, pulled out a handkerchief, and wiped the sweat from his brow. After placing his hat back on his head and giving the brim a tug to make sure his eyes were shaded, he mounted the lead mule and, with a light kick to its flanks, headed off with his pack mules.

It looked like a scene straight out of an old black-and-white Wild West movie. Later I would learn that whenever he came across what he judged was a good mineral vein, he would take samples, make a note on his topographic maps, and place claim papers in a metal pipe-tobacco can and insert it into a cone-shaped pile of rocks to mark the location. He would ride back to the pick-up point and, once back in town, take the samples to an assayer to be tested. If the results looked promising and he wanted to keep the claim, he would then have to perform further assessment per federal regulations, which required digging a hole of a certain minimum volume and providing evidence of a minimum cost in labor no later than September 1 of that year.

Milton had staked out several mining claims for copper in the popular prospecting area of the Galiuro Mountains east of Mammoth, Arizona. (I have no idea how many total claims Milton staked out, but I can tell you that we eventually worked over sixty claims.) It was June 1949, and he had less than three months to get the assessment work done. If you need to dig holes in the side of a mountain lickety-split, what do you do? You hire three teenagers who have more brawn than brains and are looking for a way to make a quick buck. My grandpa's stepsons Andrew and Lawrence and I got the job.

MORE FUN WITH DYNAMITE

Andrew, Lawrence, and I set up a base camp just off the end of a federal dirt road, about twenty feet from a small stream and a quarter of a mile southeast of the claims. We slept on folding canvas cots in a ten-by-fifteen-foot tent and built a fire pit nearby for cooking the food stored in a locked wooden box. A small tent under a mesquite tree about ten feet from the main tent held the dynamite, blasting caps, and fuses. In theory, this separation was for our safety, but if all that dynamite had gone off at once, we would have been goners regardless.

Our morning routine consisted of fetching water from the nearby stream, cooking and eating breakfast, then loading up one gunnysack with dynamite, another with the blasting caps and fuses along with our lunch (remember, we were three teenagers, burning up six thousand to eight thousand calories a day), a couple of the canvas bags that held our water, the tools, and a shotgun in case we ran into rattlesnakes. Yes, there were rattlesnakes.

We were paid $50 per claim. Our job was to drill several twenty-inch-deep, one-and-a-half-inch-diameter holes that could hold at least two sticks of dynamite around the vein. We drilled with a four-foot-long bit that had a star chisel on one end and a flat head on the other, what miners call a "bull prick." One of us would hold the drill bit and twist it back and forth while another pounded it with a sixteen-pound sledgehammer. We didn't have power tools—we were the power.

When the holes were finished, we'd put in a couple of sticks of dynamite with blasting caps and a foot-and-a-half-long fuse in each hole. Then we would light the fuse and run like hell. After the dust settled, we'd use a pick, shovel, and our hands to clean out the rock fragments.

We soon discovered that the more dynamite we used, the fewer rocks and boulders we had to move. As our efficiency improved, we were able to do two and a half to three claims a day, earning forty to fifty dollars each per day. That was big money in those days for a grown man, let alone a teenager. (My dad was making about fifteen dollars a day at that time.)

This method for increasing efficiency quickly dwindled our supply of dynamite, and I was elected to drive to the copper mine and smelter in Mammoth, even though I was only fifteen and didn't have a driver's license. Being underage and unlicensed had never stopped me before.

Inside the store, I approached the female clerk, who was wearing a long dress under a dark-tan apron and looked to be about my mom's age. "What can I help you with?" she asked, cutting to the chase.

"I need blasting caps, fuses, and dynamite," I told her. "Oh, and we'll need one of those . . . drill rods, the ones with the star bit on the end?"

"Fred!" she yelled, turning toward the warehouse in back. "Bring me a four-foot bull prick!"

I was so embarrassed that I wanted to run and hide. She didn't even notice. "Keep the blasting caps on the floorboard in the cab and the dynamite in the back of the truck, you hear?" she said as I paid for our supplies. This was clearly a woman who could hold her own, a necessary trait in a mining town.

By the end of the summer, I'd earned enough money to buy a car when I turned sixteen in November (and became a legitimate driver). Later I heard that Milton had sold the mining claims to a group of Texas oil millionaires. A few months after that, Arvilla, Milton and Irene's daughter, pulled up to the house to drop off her mom and found a couple of men forcing a handcuffed Milton into the back seat of a black sedan. She parked with a screech and jumped out, but the sedan sped off before she could reach it. Irene got their license plate number, and Arvilla ran into the house and called the Arizona Highway Patrol, which managed to stop the car before it went across New Mexico and over the state line into Texas. They returned with a free Milton and reported that the men in the black sedan were Texas Rangers with a Texas warrant against Milton for falsifying assaying records. It turned out that his assay samples were obtained by what is called "nutpicking," taking the mineral sample directly and only out of the mineral vein. Without a sample of the bed surrounding the vein that has to be removed to extract the ore, you get a false estimated cost for mining the ore.

I never learned the outcome of this little showdown, or whether the Texas Rangers' claims were true. Milton wasn't the kind of guy you'd ask about such a thing. So I stayed in the dark about the possibility of my own participation in any unsavory ventures, which, because I hadn't known and couldn't do anything about it anyway, was probably for the best. The next thing I knew, Milton had moved on from prospecting to building a motel.

ALWAYS HAVE AN ESCAPE ROUTE

I'll admit that my primary reason for moving back to Mesa was the lack of girls in California. Cathy had gone off to college, bringing my family church's teenage female population down to three. Plus I was already in Arizona, and I knew that I'd be given more independence if I lived with my aunt Falene and her husband, Jearl, for the year.

We had a deal—I would babysit their daughters, five-year-old Jearldene and three-year-old Judy, every Saturday night or find (and fund) a substitute babysitter, and they'd let me do pretty much whatever I wanted. Thinking back, I'm surprised by how much freedom I was granted. My family as well as other adults seemed to forget that I was only fifteen, or that having some structure or boundaries might have been beneficial.

Per usual, school bored me from day one. What does a bored kid with little supervision and a love of noise and high stakes do? Get up to mischief, that's what. By this point, I was feeling confident about my dynamite skills, and I thought I'd share the joy of explosion with my fellow high schoolers. (If I'd been going to school in today's environment of justified fear about school shootings, I like to think that I would have made a different choice.)

With my buddy Denzel Arrington, whom I knew from school years past in Mesa, I filled balloons with two parts hydrogen gas and one part oxygen, then tied them with strings that had been soaked in potassium nitrate and dried for fuses. These we called "booms."

I'd discovered a ladder to the roof backstage in the auditorium when I was a stagehand for a school play freshman year. It went up to the fly loft, then extended to the ceiling and, beyond that, a hatch that opened to the roof. Up there, above our classmates milling around in the courtyard, we lit the fuses one at a time and released the booms so they would rise up and float over the group. If someone had looked up in that moment, they might have thought to themselves, *Oh, what pretty balloons.* No one did look up—that is, until the booms started exploding with giant pops. More than one startled person threw their books in the air at the sound.

Laughing maniacally, my friend and I raced to the hatch toward the ladder. We hadn't thought ahead about this being the only way down, or that the principal surely knew his own territory well enough to pinpoint where the booms were coming from and realize there was no alternative escape route. When we got to the ladder and looked down, there he was waiting, wagging his index finger at us, with that "gotcha" look on his face that I'd become familiar with two years earlier. "I knew it was you, Bryce," he called up, shaking his head.

Our punishment was a three-day suspension, and we were required to make up any assignments we missed. In other words, we got a three-day vacation. Some punishment!

INTEGRATION

Don't think that all my junior year entailed was boredom and misbehavior. That fall, a small black high school about five miles away on the other side of Tempe burned down. We were told that the fire had started by spontaneous combustion, that supposedly the janitor had left a pile of oily dust mops in a closet that had somehow caught fire. Luckily, no one was hurt.

This was five years before the Supreme Court's 1954 landmark decision in *Brown vs. Board of Education*, in which it was decided that separate was not equal, and that segregation in public schools was unconstitutional. Even after that ruling, many states, particularly in the South, resisted integration, and it would be many more years before the Civil Rights Act of 1964 and the Elementary and Secondary

Education Act of 1965 made discrimination illegal and put funding toward incentivizing integration in schools.[5] Many would argue that today's schools have maintained segregation by way of housing and economic policies that bar black and brown kids from the same opportunities as their white peers. Many would argue that we still have a long way to go.

Way back in 1949, Arizona was still one of the strictest Western states regarding segregation, and state law allowed the school districts to choose whether to open their doors to nonwhite kids.[6] Many districts simply turned down the burned school's request for admitting their students until it could be rebuilt. Mesa High School had already begun taking some small measures toward integration—out of almost a thousand students in my yearbook, there are a handful of black and Latino kids—and so Mesa High was the first and only to accept this dispossessed student body.

The administration choreographed a way to help the new kids get settled. This intentional, organized welcoming showed that we as a school wanted to make integration go as smoothly as possible and also to endure long-term. The administration assigned honor roll students and other students who could afford to miss three days of classes to be greeters and mentors. Each of us received a sheet of white construction paper with a student's name handwritten on it.

I remember the day when the yellow school bus pulled up in front of the school and thirty or forty black students

---

5. Richard D. Kahlenberg, Halley Potter, Kimberly Quick, "Segregation Is Preventable. Congress Just Isn't Trying." The Atlantic, April 18,2019, https://www.theatlantic.com/ideas/archive/2019/04/school-integration -over-compensatory-education/587407/.

6. Jan Cleere, "Western Women: Teacher Set High Expectations for Black Students," Arizona Daily Star, March 14, 2016, Tucson.com (website), https://tucson.com/news/local/western-women-teacher-set-high -expectations-for-black-students/article_5ec390c9-a049-5f9f-a072 -f63f7a051dbd.html.

disembarked. I looked down at the piece of paper in my hand—a boy named Albert was to be my charge.

Like us, these students had already started classes, so they were given a corresponding schedule for their new school. All of us mentors chaperoned them for the day, orienting them to their new classrooms and making them feel comfortable and welcome. "This is Albert," I said to any friend or acquaintance we happened to pass in the hall or sat next to in class. The teachers had also been instructed to ask each new student to stand up and introduce themself. I could tell that Albert was nervous, but he had a big voice and a warm demeanor, and as far as I could tell everyone was friendly to him.

Albert and I had a special lunch with the other mentors and mentees, courtesy of the school. It was during this meal that I learned that Albert had played on his school football team. He was assigned PE last period, along with all the other athletes, because this allowed the class to extend an hour for two total hours of practice. Right away Albert's football talent and skill were evident, and he made the team. We became buddies on campus and on the football field, and we often goofed around on the bus going home after practice. He had a good, if somewhat crass, sense of humor.

People are often surprised by my experience of integration at Mesa High. Most are more familiar with horror stories, of those photos of white students and adults terrorizing black children as they entered Little Rock Central High School in 1957. I want folks to know that not everyone or everywhere was like that—there were some who were open to integration simply because it was the right thing to do.

CHOOSE ICE CREAM, NOT HATE

Yotes was a neighborhood boy whom today we'd call "intellectually disabled." (Looking back, I think "Yotes" was a nickname, and maybe not a nice one; I never did learn his real name.) He lived somewhere between the high school and my house. Often, when he saw me walking to or from school, he would call out, "Herb, wait! Wait!" I'd wait until he caught up with me, and together we'd walk, passing Dairy Queen and stopping so I could buy him an ice cream cone. Yotes really loved ice cream.

I realize now that Yotes probably didn't go to school. They didn't have special education back then, or even much patience for different styles of learning. I think he just hung around outside because he was a friendly person and liked to be with people. Most folks would stop and say hello before continuing on their way.

I do remember that a few times his mother came running after him, calling out, *"Pára, tienes que volver a casa! Tienes que volver a casa."* ("Stop, you have to go home. You have to come home.")

"It's OK," I'd tell her. "Let him walk with me up to the Dairy Queen. You can come too, and I'll buy all of us ice cream cones." She accompanied us a couple of times, thanking me for the ice cream and for being good to her son. Then she would take her son's hand and lead him home.

I considered Yotes my friend. He was good company and a nice guy, and this, along with his disability, made him vulnerable to the cruelty of others. I remember one lunchtime coming outside to him singing "Blue Moon" on the side lawn of Old Main, a group of students gathered around. The kids were egging him on, laughing, teasing and making fun of him while he smiled innocently, happy to have the attention.

I'm glad that he didn't know what they were really doing, that he was the butt of a joke, but back then it upset me so much that I elbowed my way through the crowd and gently grabbed his arm. "Hey, Yotes," I said. "How about we go get some ice cream? I'll buy you a double scoop."

Junior year was a big year for my education about bigotry and discrimination. For whatever reason, I just couldn't stomach hostility directed at people for things they had no control over, like skin color or intellectual ability or familial religion. *Why,* I asked myself, *do people care so much about these attributes, and use them to cause harm and spread hate? Didn't anyone ever teach them manners? Don't they have anything better to do?* These questions and this attitude would get me into trouble later in life, like the time I offered a young black mother my seat on the bus, a year or two before Rosa Parks refused to leave the whites-only section on her bus in Montgomery, Alabama. Or when I was at a hospital and caused a stir by offering to donate my blood to a black stabbing victim who'd just been wheeled in on a gurney. Or when I drank from the coloreds-only water fountain at Woolworth. The white bus driver and white nurses and white salespeople, among others, were not happy about my racial line crossing.

The moment that stands out most in my mind is when a friend and I hitched a ride with a middle-aged black man from Memphis to Mississippi. An hour or so into the ride, the driver took a little green book out of the glove box.

"Can you flip through and find a nearby gas station in there?" he asked. "I need to pee."

"We just passed a gas station," I said, swiveling in my seat to look at the rearview mirror. "Why don't we turn around? Won't take but a minute."

The man glanced over at us, a couple of blond, blue-eyed, clean-cut white boys. "I'm not welcome at that gas station," he said. "If I were to pull over and let my dog out on the side of the road to pee, no one would think twice. But if I did the same, the police would have me in handcuffs fast as you please. That book is a guidebook for black people in this area—where it's safe to get gas, go to the bathroom, grab a bite to eat, that sort of thing."

I was completely floored. I'd spent my whole life wandering wherever I felt like, and I'd never given a second thought to whether I'd be welcome, let alone whether my presence might come with significant danger. I felt comfortable, well, everywhere. To me, the world was a wide-open urinal! I didn't need any safety guidebook for finding a place to pee, and I'd never considered that someone else—that many other people—did. The new awareness of how my relative place in the world compared to that of the black truck driver really shook me up. It just seemed so . . . unfair.

ANGER MANAGEMENT FOR DUMMIES: YOU CAN'T UNDENT A DENT

Shortly after my sixteenth birthday, I bought my first car, a black 1941 Ford Club Coupe, from the man who owned the local auto body shop. The car's paint job looked practically brand new, gorgeous and flawless and shining like it had just come off the production line. In my eyes, it was the most beautiful car on the road, and I gave it the royal treatment that it deserved, hand washing and waxing it every Saturday morning until it gleamed, scrubbing the whitewalls of the tires until they were spotless. I kept a whisk broom and a special polishing cloth in the glove box just in case a speck of dirt or lint or dust dared to take up residence on the seats or floorboards. It was so clean and shiny that on a sunny day, you practically needed sunglasses just to look at it.

I had driven to Fontana, California, to show off my beloved car to my mom and dad. Between Indio and Banning there was a big desert windstorm, which covered it with a thick layer of dust, transforming my black beauty into a dull-gray dirt box. It needed a lot of tender loving care to restore it to its former glory, so I got up early the morning after my arrival to perform my Saturday-morning ritual.

Just as I finished wiping the very last speck of dirt away, my uncle Talmage, who was living with my folks at the time, appeared and proceeded to inflate my ego by telling me what a great job I had done. "I love your car," he said as my cheeks turned pink with pride. He paused while I waited for his next compliment. "Tell you what," he continued, "how about I let you drive us to Los Angeles to see the Ice Follies this afternoon?"

Of course, I jumped at the chance, not realizing that I had just been suckered into not only providing transportation but paying for gas. At around a quarter per gallon I wasn't too concerned, but it was a hundred-mile round trip.

We arrived with the car's shine mostly intact but found that parking was scarce around the ice arena. I parked several blocks away in an area that today, after sixty-odd years of driving experience, I would have avoided. But what did I know back then?

After the show, as we walked to the car, rehashing the hilarity of the Frick and Frack comedic ice-skating duo, I had no idea that one of the best educational moments of my life was right around the corner.

Even from a distance, I could see a brand-new dent in the back fender of my black beauty. Some maniac must have backed into it and then just took off! My car, my perfect, beautiful car, was now ruined, a wreck, a testament to the futility of all things! I ran up to get a better look at the destruction, and then rage overtook me and I was shaking my fist, stomping my feet, yelling my head off. I'll spare you the details, but I will just say that I screamed some obscenities that would have made a merchant marine blush, that would have compelled my mother to wash my mouth out with a bar of Fels-Naptha laundry soap.

After a moment, Talmage called out, "Herb! Come over here." I didn't respond; I was still caught up in my little temper tantrum. "HERB!" Talmage bellowed, "COME HERE!"

I stopped yelling, but my fists were clenched and my heart was racing as I turned to see what he wanted. "Come here and stand where I'm standing," he said in a voice that was quieter and therefore more authoritative.

I walked over, still mad as hell, and stood next to him. Talmage said, "Stay right here and let me try." He went over to the spot where I had been and started yelling, using the same swear words I'd used, plus a couple extras I'd never even heard before. He stomped his feet and beat his chest and generally looked like someone who had lost his mind. Then he stopped cold.

Turning to look at me, he again said in a calm voice, "Come here." I did. He continued, "Now, it didn't work for you, and it didn't work for me, so let's both throw a fit and see if that dent fixes itself."

He then started up again, yelling obscenities, shaking his fists, and shouting at me to join him, which I did with gusto. It didn't take more than a minute for me to see what a stupid thing we were doing. I started laughing, then Talmage started laughing, and we laughed and laughed and laughed until tears streamed down our cheeks. All the anger and profanity in the world was not going to change the situation. All our hooting and hollering might have made the dent vibrate a little, but, in the end, it was still there, just as dented as it had been before.

Fortunately, I'd bought my first insurance policy—$34, plus $2 for comprehensive coverage, with a $25 deductible—when I bought my first car. Back in Arizona the following week, I took my car to the auto body shop to be repaired. When I told the owner the story, he laughed and informed me that my insurance would take care of it and that I wouldn't even have to pay the deductible. I picked up the car a few days later. Once again, I had the most beautiful car on the road. Best of all, I'd learned one of the most valuable lessons of my life: you can get angry at life's little injustices, but it's not going to fix anything—the only thing it'll do is make you look like an idiot. The cost of tuition? The price of insurance, a hundred miles' worth of gas, and a ticket to the Ice Follies.

JUST ASK

That year, I also learned about how to interact with girls. Starting freshman year, if I was interested in a girl, I would ask her out—it was that simple, and I didn't spend a whole lot of time worrying about it beforehand. If she said yes, great. If she said no, then that was fine, too. In fact, I never felt rejected when a girl declined—it was my prerogative to ask, and it was her prerogative to answer however she might. (The only time this was a problem was when Cathy and I weren't honest and direct.) Ultimately, it came down to respect.

Because of this open mindset and casual confidence, I'd experienced my share of both yeses and noes. I'd also realized that sometimes boys didn't ask girls out if they were intimidated, assuming that, for whatever reason, the girl would likely say no. (Back then, convention had it that boys were supposed to take the active role, while girls were given the passive one.) Perhaps this "if you don't try, you won't fail" attitude saved those boys from the pain of rejection, but it probably also meant they missed out on what might have been fun dates and connections.

Joan was one of those girls who I think my fellow male students felt was out of their league. She was very pretty and well spoken, had perfect posture, and was on the path to becoming valedictorian. She was a member of the National Honor Society, a soloist in the chorus, a cellist, the first-chair violinist, and an accomplished ballerina and tennis player. Her daddy was a lawyer, and her family lived far north of "the tracks." I didn't exactly live on the wrong side of the tracks, but I did live next to them, and I was sure I would be one among many hoping for a date. Even so, I asked.

It was a surprise when I got an excited yes. My speech and drama teacher had offered me tickets to a series of concerts that included classical, chamber and symphony, jazz music, and ballet, modern dance, and jazz dance. I was the teacher's pet, and I think she recognized my curiosity about the wider world. I'd also given a speech about how real masculinity isn't threatened by washing the dishes, which won her avid approval and after which she told my female classmates, "Girls, this is the man for you!"

At first, I assumed that Joan had agreed to go out with me because of those tickets. But when I confessed that I'd thought she was out of my league and that I didn't think I had a chance, she told me that she had very few dates. I couldn't believe it, but a survey of several boys in my class yielded the same type of answers: "She's too classy for me" was a common refrain. "I'm sure she gets asked out all the time and so isn't available" was another one.

From this I learned three things: First, just ask. The worst thing that can happen is that she'll say no. Second, choose an activity that the girl will enjoy—this makes it more likely that she will say yes, and it shows that you're paying attention.

Joan and I had a fabulous time. By the time we arrived, there were no seats left, but my big sad puppy-dog eyes must have worked, because the usher let us sit in the wing. We were so close to the orchestra that we could practically see the beads of sweat on the conductor's brow. I fell in love with the music and, at the next concert, modern dance. It was my first taste of culture, and all I can say is that it woke me up.

After the show, Joan and I talked about how incredible the music was, the beauty of the sound of seventy-five instruments in perfect coordination, all the way home. From this I learned my third part of the lesson: listen.

FIRST LOVE

I already knew that I was going to be moving away when I first laid eyes on Ethelyn. My uncle Jearl was completing his teaching degree and planning to take Falene and their girls to California, and the Mesa school board had recently passed a rule that anyone living outside the district would have to pay tuition for public school. These two factors would make it impossible for me to stay. Besides, I was used to moving nearly every year.

But love has nothing to do with logistics. I had been walking Ann to class when this doe-eyed, dark-haired girl approached. "This is Ethelyn," Ann said, and it was like in the movies where the whole world disappears and all you can see is that one person. They kept talking as we continued down the hall, and then somehow Ann just sort of disappeared and there I was, walking Ethelyn to class.

Looking back, I guess I would have to call it love at first sight. My feelings for her certainly defied my usual pattern—I met and dated all kinds of attractive, nice girls, but I thought of them as girl friends and wasn't looking for a girlfriend. In part that had to do with the fact that I was always leaving and therefore always avoiding, consciously or not, getting too attached. More than one girl had told me that I was incapable of love, but none of them had stopped my heart the way Ethelyn did. She was smart and a little bit shy and beautiful in a way that was wholly her own, and she just had that something about her, that indescribable something. All I wanted was to get to know her.

I began to orient my day around walking her to class. One morning, we passed a hedge of orange blossoms in bloom, and I stopped and picked a flower for her, just as my dad and grandpa had taught me. She smiled when I handed it to her, and when I returned at the end of the period to walk her to her next class, she was wearing the blossom in one of the buttonholes of her sweater. I hoped that meant she liked me, too.

With the co-ed dance coming up, rumor had it that two girls were planning to ask me, and I set about avoiding them like the plague while going out of my way to put myself in Ethelyn's sight line. For the first time, I was nervous. For the first time, I was the one waiting.

After what seemed like an eternity, she asked me. From there on out we spent every free moment together. She was the only one I wanted to be with. But even as I was falling head over heels, in the back of my mind I knew that soon I would have to say goodbye.

Her dad, like most fathers of the girls I knew, would have been more than a little overjoyed to see the last of me. He'd caught on to my habit of unscrewing the light bulb in the porch light upon arrival so that we wouldn't be seen during our good-night kiss, then screwing it back in once Ethelyn had gone inside. "You're not Romeo and Juliet," he once said to me after I brought his daughter home after curfew. As I mentioned earlier, this kind of parental disapproval usually has the opposite of its intended effect, though I knew all he was trying to do was protect her, to make sure she wouldn't get involved in something that might stop her from going to college. He was wrong in at least one respect: we were like Romeo and Juliet, in that our romance was destined to end too soon.

Before this, I always knew instinctively the difference between right and wrong. Wrong was making fun of a kid because he's not as smart as you, or lying to a girl, or talking back to your mother. This was the first time that I truly didn't know which was which. Not being honest with Ethelyn about how I felt seemed cruel, but telling her my true feelings and then leaving seemed like a terribly cruel thing to do, too. My grandmother had taught me to avoid hurting others whenever possible. But what if, no matter what you did, someone was going to get hurt?

One night, on the way home from a date with Ethelyn at the movies, I passed the high school. Sitting down on the front steps, I let my brain and heart have a long conversation.

Tell her how you feel, said my heart. *You'll only hurt her more when you leave if you do,* countered my brain.

In the end, my brain won. I never told her I loved her. We said a quiet goodbye at the end of the school year, and that was that. I have never forgotten her.

FIRE DRILL

While in the school office first thing on a warm Tuesday morning that spring, I overheard the assistant principal telling a student helper to type up notices for the faculty that announced a fire drill during fourth period on Thursday. Of course, right away my brain started storming. That was the period that my friend Lee and I were in chemistry. Two bored and overly self-confident boys with access to chemicals, plus a fire drill . . . what could go wrong?

The chemistry teacher, Mr. Whitehead, had unknowingly planted the seed of an idea earlier that semester, when he'd done a demonstration that entailed a smoke bomb. After the demo, I'd even told Lee that it would be fun to set one of those off during a fire drill. Now, weeks later, that seed was about to sprout.

Wednesday was lab day. The lecture room and lab were side by side, and usually Mr. Whitehead would explain the instructions for the experiment in the lecture room before moving the class into the lab. He would then walk around the lab to check that we had set up everything correctly, and if we had, he'd give us a nod of approval. After he made his rounds, he would return to his stool at the demonstration desk and grade papers while the students ran their experiments. Occasionally he would get up and walk around the lab so that we could ask questions.

That Wednesday, Lee and I used our lab time to get ready for the next day. I'd brought sugar from home, which we mixed with potassium nitrate in a large porcelain-evaporating dish. While Mr. Whitehead was grading papers, we placed it on a heating stand and inserted an inch-long piece of magnesium ribbon for the fuse. Once the process was complete, we snuck it into the chemistry storage closet and hid it on a shelf. Despite what they might tell you, teachers do not have eyes in the back of their heads, and Mr. Whitehead was none the wiser.

The next day, when the fire alarm sounded, Lee and I ducked into the chemistry storage room and waited until everyone was gone. The lab was perfect for our prank because it was at the end of the hall, with windows on one side and in the back. The building didn't have air-conditioning, so on a warm day like this one, the windows were open, and there was a big fan on a stand to both cool the room and blow chemical fumes out. Hunched over so we wouldn't be seen by those who were already gathered in the schoolyard, Lee pushed Mr. Whitehead's stool over to the window, and I carried over the bowl and heating stand, set them up on the stool, and lit the magnesium ribbon fuse. Still hunched over, we backed up and turned the fan on.

Suddenly, we heard students yelling, "It's in the chem room! Fire in the chem room!" Unable to resist witnessing the chaos we'd created, we popped our heads up so that our eyes were just above the window ledge. It was less than a second later that an eagle-eyed teacher shouted, "Someone's in the room!"

And just like that, the jig was up. I was great at pulling pranks but damn poor at planning escape routes.

The principal's voice sounded almost resigned. "OK, Bryce," he said through the door to the chem room a minute later. "Come on out and bring your partner in crime with you."

Lee and I looked at one another. He shrugged and opened the door. We left the room, hanging our heads as we stood in front of the principal—even though I wasn't really ashamed, I knew it would be wise to act the part.

"We were about to call the fire department," the principal said. "Lucky one of the teachers recognized you when you were peering out the window." He sighed. "I'm glad that it's close to the end of the year. If you'd spent the same amount of time studying as you do making trouble, you'd be an honor student."

"Sir," I said, raising my eyes to his, "I'm already an honor student." Lee sniggered.

"Oh, for Pete's sake. At least I only have one more year with you."

"I have good news for you, then. I'm moving to Compton, California, this summer."

"There is a God," the principal said, practically dropping to his knees with gratitude. "That's the best news I've had all week."

SEWERS IN SUMMERTIME

I finished my junior year mid-May, just as Jearl received his bachelor's degree in elementary education. With a diploma and a teaching contract from the Fontana School District in hand, he was ready to pack up and move to California. He and my aunt Falene wanted to make sure they had a home for their two young daughters before they moved all their belongings, and I was still working at Wright's Super Market, so I stayed behind while they figured things out, since the rent had been paid till the end of May. After they came back to pack up, I moved in with my step-uncle Lawrence.

After Grandpa and Lola retired and moved to California, Lawrence, Andrew, and I converted a shed into a single room and a three-quarters bath, with the blessing of the widow who owned it. Lawrence was living there while going to college, and his rent included room and board. While Jearl, Falene, and the girls were in California, Lawrence suggested that we three guys start a subcontracting business, and that I move in with him once Falene and family were gone. I gave my notice to Wright's soon after they packed up and left, and moved in with Lawrence; we split the rent, and I paid full board.

That spring of 1950, the city of Mesa had extended their sewer system to service a group of houses to the west. The local plumbers were charging two dollars a foot to connect the homeowners' sewer systems to the city's system, and Lawrence, after doing the calculations, convinced us that we three strong and hardworking guys could do the same job for a dollar a foot. The plumbers were using backhoes and bulldozers that tore up lawns, and he argued we could sweeten the deal by doing it manually with pick and shovels. Not only would we be charging half the price, we would be preserving the homeowners' grass.

Soon enough we were going full steam ahead; we even had a waiting list. One of the owners of Mesa Plumbing, who also happened to be my second cousin, got his nose bent out of shape over our undercutting, and he convinced the city that only a licensed plumber could lay the pipes correctly. He must have had a friend or two in high places, because soon thereafter the city red tagged us.

Our customers were not pleased. Mesa Plumbing approached them with their two-dollars-per-foot price, which they refused. "Our cesspool is working fine," they said. "Besides, you tear up the lawns."

His hands tied, my cousin approached us with an offer. "I'll hire you," he said, "so you'll be covered by my license. All you got to do is pay me fifty cents per foot."

"So let me get this straight," I said. "We do all the work, *and* we pay you?"

My second cousin shrugged. "Yup, sounds about right."

That didn't sound very fair to us, but we'd been red tagged, and this, it seemed, was the only way around it. "We made an agreement with our customers, but if we stay at a dollar per foot, we'll barely break even," Lawrence said. He paused, then continued: "Tell you what. If you can get them to pay a dollar fifty per foot, we'll do the work for the people we already signed." All but two customers agreed to these new terms.

A week before we finished, Andrew's former employer approached him about doing some subcontracting work. He needed help installing drywall, roofing, and sheeting exterior walls. Sheetrock, also known as drywall, was a new innovation in home building, and because putting it up required less labor, houses with sheetrock could be sold for a lower price. (The plasterers' union encouraged the idea that plaster was more sound with the slogan "Just Knock on the Walls.") Eventually homebuyers caught on: If you have to knock on the walls to tell the difference, is it really worth paying 20 percent more for plaster?

At the end of summer, Lawrence went back to Arizona State, Andrew stayed on to continue working full time as a contractor, and I headed to Compton with a pocketful of money and high school nearly done.

STEPPING INTO THE FUTURE

Perhaps it was that times and styles were changing, or that I'd become more aware of social norms in my Mormon small town in Arizona, but the move to Compton, California, was a big culture shock, bigger than any I'd experienced previously. The boys in Mesa wore their hair cut short and neatly parted to one side, while the boys of Compton sported duck-tail pompadours, with a big swish up from the crown of the head and tapering to a point at the back of the neck. Think Dick Van Dyke versus Elvis Presley. Many carried a pack of cigarettes rolled up in their T-shirt sleeves and belonged to gangs you could identify by their black leather jackets and black-and-white high-top sneakers.

The girls of Mesa also held to the more-conservative hair and wardrobe styles, while the girls of Compton grew their hair long and wore dresses and sweaters that were more form-fitting. You could identify girl cliques by the brands of clothing and shoes each member wore. I was used to approaching a girl in a more-formal manner when on a date, always coming to the door and meeting the parents before taking her out. A respectable Mesa girl would never ask a boy out; in Compton, girls did plenty of inviting. And most boys just pulled up to the curb in front of their dates' houses and honked the horn rather than coming to the door.

I quickly realized that living in Mesa had been like living in a time warp. The Mormon monoculture restrained society within a narrow range of acceptability. Though I missed some aspects of general courtesy and chivalry, and I was not interested in joining any gangs, I was happy with the openness and permissiveness of my new school. There, I felt it was easier for me to just be me.

For the most part, I focused on school, after-school part-time jobs, and football. I got a job at the local drugstore, which had the best cigar selection in town. I would place a wedding band the drugstore manager had given me on my ring finger before every shift, hoping to pass for twenty-two so that I could sell liquor and tobacco. I was only sixteen going on seventeen, but people had always thought I looked older, and now was no exception. I was also entrusted with the responsibility of selling condoms, which were kept in a locked drawer under the counter. When a customer asked for this product, usually in a whisper, I had to unlock the drawer and place the condoms in a paper bag before handing it over. It was all very hush-hush.

At my other job, the Standard Oil service station, I filled gas tanks, or lifted the hood to check the oil, water levels, the brake and transmission fluid, and the fan belt and battery connections, or inflated the tires, or used a little whisk broom to sweep the floorboards, all in my clean white uniform. We also washed and waxed. (The first *Back to the Future* movie's portrayal of 1950s service stations is pretty realistic.)

Even though the Mesa team, with me playing as offensive pulling guard and defensive linebacker, had won the Arizona State Championship the previous year, it took a lot of work to convince the Compton coach to let me try out for a spot on the team. He already had a full lineup, but eventually he let me play the positions of outside linebacker and backup offensive guard. Homework and after-school work and sports (and, of course, dating) kept me very busy that fall, especially when the football team made it to the Southern California Championship and won. For the first time in my life, I was staying out of trouble.

So I was surprised when the principal sent a note asking me to stop by his office at the end of the first semester, right before winter break. It had been ages since I'd even thought about setting off a boom or making a smoke bomb! I racked my brain, trying to remember if I'd pulled some small prank during the last few months, but I came up with nothing.

"Come on in, Herb," the principal said when I knocked on the door. "Have a seat." I looked around while he opened a drawer and shuffled through some papers. His office was the same as all the principals' offices I'd ever been in—mostly beige and bland and tidy, with some trophies lining the windowsill, and books placed neatly on the bookshelf. Outside, palm trees stood tall along the sidewalk. Finally, after a minute, the principal said, "Congratulations," and I turned back toward him with a start. "Here's your diploma." He reached across the desk and handed me a piece of paper. "You have just graduated from high school."

I was shocked. "I . . . Are you sure?"

"Yes, I'm sure."

I was at a loss for words. This was completely unexpected. "Well," I said, and then paused to clear my throat. "Thank you."

"You don't need to thank me. You've earned it. Now go enroll in college where you belong."

And that was that. I was done with high school. Like so many graduates before and after, suddenly the prospect of a future, with all its unknowns, appeared before me.

BETWEEN THE PAST AND THE FUTURE

With school no longer taking up my time, I could devote all my energy to making plans and saving money. I knew that if

I wanted to go to college, I would have to find a way to pay for it myself. Neither of my parents had graduated from high school, and higher education just wasn't on their radar. But ever since science class with Mr. Kühn in the fifth grade, I'd known that I wanted to be a scientist. And being a scientist required having a college education.

Shortly after my early graduation, I was talking on the phone to my Mesa buddy Denzel. He told me that a number of players from the Mesa football team had received scholarships to Arizona State College. "If you'd stayed here," Denzel said, "you would have probably gotten one, too."

That got me thinking. A scholarship! That would be the ticket to my going to college. Right away I reached out to Coach Brady, the Mesa football coach, who said he would be glad to write me a letter of recommendation based on my performance on the team junior year. I also contacted the coach at Compton, who agreed to do the same. But instead of having them send the letters to ASC, I asked them to write to Brigham Young University. (For the life of me, I don't remember why I chose BYU instead of ASC. Perhaps I missed the comfort and familiarity of living with Mormons.) A few weeks later, the BYU coach offered me a tryout for a football scholarship.

I spent the summer working on my uncle Grant's bee farm in Mesa, quickly learning from experience that bees have a thing for bananas, bright T-shirts, and scented aftershave. I got enough bee stings the first week to develop immunity (to the poison, not the pain). I mostly removed, melted, and filtered wax from old honeycomb frames and transported hives to farms that had rented them. Of course, I wouldn't be me if that didn't involve tipping over enough hives to send a hundred thousand bees into a frenzy, or getting blamed for a bee invasion at a service station in Tucson. It was a sticky, sweet, and stingy summer.

In mid-August, I loaded up my car for the drive up to BYU, stopping for a visit with my football buddies who were now practicing for the season at ASC in Flagstaff. The afternoon of my arrival, Denzel took me along to football practice to meet his coach. The coach took one look at me and said, "Would you like to try out for the team?"

"I have a conditional offer from BYU," I said. "Tryouts begin next Tuesday."

"That's OK," said the coach. "How about you suit up and practice with the team? Just for fun."

I must have been doing pretty well, because the coach had me play different positions so he could assess my strengths and weaknesses. At the end of the practice, as the rest of the team started to head to the locker room, he called me over.

"Take a lap and have a shower," he said, "then stop by my office for a chat."

At this point, I still wasn't all that interested in playing for ASC. I was pretty sure I could make the team at BYU, and since I didn't really know the difference between the colleges, that was good enough for me. That is, until I was crossing the road between the playing field and the locker room and heard a horn honk. A car with four girls in it pulled up.

One girl poked her head out the rear window. "Hi, Herb," she said. I could tell right away that she was one of those people who was just plain nice to her very core. "I'm Jenny. I'm a good friend of Denzel's. He told me about you, and I thought I'd introduce myself. Come on over here so we can say hi." Jenny and I would go on to become great friends.

The coach offered me a full scholarship, including tuition, books, and fees, room and board, and a job in the greenhouse. That, with Denzel and the promise of new friendships to come, made it impossible for me to refuse. I enrolled in Arizona State College. I was on my way to becoming a scientist. I was about to begin a new life.

EPILOGUE

Life's Little Rules

Fifty-one years after I finished high school, I was invited to give the commencement speeches at Shorecrest High School's and Shorewood High School's graduation. It was 2001, and five hundred bright young adults in Shoreline, Washington, were ready to take the helm of the new century. I can only imagine how vastly different the lives of the graduating class were from my own; but even though technologies, social norms, and hairstyles change, people tend to stay the same.

I was a spring chicken at a mere sixty-eight years old at the time. Still, I'd managed to collect a few tidbits of wisdom along the way, and I shared them with pride and with hope. Now, as my ninetieth birthday approaches, I will share them with you.

Look after the wellbeing of your body *and* your mind.
Taking care of your body is the easy part—eat the right foods without overdoing it, take your vitamins, exercise regularly, don't smoke. The hard part, the part we tend to overlook, is taking care of the mind.

Both mind and body need nourishment and exercise. Read widely and often. Don't limit yourself to books that support only your established philosophy; read the opposite point of view, read about topics you know little about, read for the joy of reading. Learn about people and ideas not just from books but from other people. Remain open and accessible, and travel as far and wide as you can. Head for the back roads, not just the shopping. Experience other cultures. The more you learn about others, the more you will understand where you fit into the scheme of life.

Include lots and lots of humor in your life. Humor is nourishment for the body, the mind, and the soul.

Life is too important to take it too seriously.
Remember that we are only here on earth for a short visit. One hundred years from now, you will be gone and there will be all new people here, living their own lives just as you lived yours. Turn off your cell phone and take off your watch when you go on vacation. Skip rocks across the water. Give your family your undivided attention. Teach as many little kids as you can the proper way to jump in a mud puddle—you know, with both feet.

The gift of happiness belongs to those who unwrap it.
There is no way to happiness . . . happiness is the way. Find work that you enjoy and that's worthy of your talents. Don't get so caught up in the daily grind that you never

create time for fun and pleasure. Making happiness is your responsibility.

Happiness doesn't come from possessions, power, or prestige but from relationships with people you love and respect.

Love people more than things. The best things in life are not things. Remember, he who dies with the most toys still dies. As former First Lady and Secretary of State Hillary Clinton said, "Don't confuse having a career with having a life. They are not the same." Material things don't last, and status is fleeting, but the love you give to your family will never be erased from their hearts.

There are two ways to get rich—either you can make more, or you can require less.

Live below your means, and never compare yourself to your friends. There is a big difference between the appearance of wealth and the feeling of wealth. Figure out what's worth spending money on, and forget the rest. Start saving for retirement when you receive your first paycheck, and add to your savings account every payday thereafter, even if it's only a dollar. Manage your resources wisely.

Commit to the right person.

This decision will determine 90 percent of your happiness or misery. Love is not the same thing as lust: lust fades over time while love grows stronger with every passing year. Love means respecting a person for what they are, not what you want them to be. Remember, nobody belongs to you.

If you have children, when you have raised them, stop raising them.

Don't expect life to be fair.
Good things happen to both good people and bad people. The reverse is also true—bad things happen to good people and bad people. That's life.

Learn from the mistakes of others—you won't live long enough to make them all yourself—without blaming them. Everyone makes mistakes, and every mistake is an opportunity to learn something. Take responsibility for every area of your life.

Prioritize.
As Harvey Mackay said, "Decide what your priorities are and how much time you'll spend on them. If you don't, someone else will." You have to choose to take control of your life. You can either be as happy as you want to be or as miserable as you want to be—it's up to you.

Service is the rent we pay for living.
Give back to your community with your time and your money. As you make your way through life, leave a trail worth following. Sir Winston Churchill said, "We make a living by what we get . . . We make a life by what we give."

You will make a difference—make your impact on the world positive.

Practice being the best self you can be.
Twenty-five hundred years ago, Euripides said, "There is just one life for each of us: our own." If that's the case—and, as far as I can tell, it is—spend your one life learning, growing, working to be the best version of yourself. When you look back on your life, what do you want to see?

ACKNOWLEDGMENTS

A very sincere thank-you to Anna Katz. She turned a novice's attempt to write this memoir into the real thing. I lived the life, but she brought life to my stories. I am grateful for her talents and proud of her work. Without Anna, you would not be reading this book.

Another thank-you goes to Patti Giboney. For years, during conversations after dinner, while Patti, Rick, and Gloria gracefully listened to my youthful adventures, Patti would comment, "You have to write that book." The answer to your goading over the years is "Thanks for the prodding! Here it is!"

An apology to my wife, Gloria, who benevolently listened to me retell the stories over and over to different friends and relatives and pretended that she was enjoying them. There cannot be any greater love.

BOOK CLUB QUESTIONS

1. Herb displays a real thirst for knowledge about his birth-place. Have you ever been interested in where you were born? What do you think your birthplace says about you and your family?
2. Herb spends the vast majority of his childhood moving from town to town. Did you move often as a child and as a result have to frequently switch schools? What effect did this have on your upbringing?
3. The Bryces' extended family members often lived with each other at various stages in their lives. What effect do you think this had on Herb as he was growing up? Is this something that you also experienced during your childhood or are currently experiencing now?
4. Strong work ethic is a pervasive theme throughout *Me and the Cottonwood Tree*. Herb first learns about hard work from his grandpa. Where did you learn your values about hard work from as a child?
5. Dating as a teenager is an issue that most of us (and especially those of us with teenaged children) have faced. What do you think are the pros and cons of the type of casual "friend" dating that Herb participated in through most of high school?

6. Taking a stand for what is right is something that Herb has done multiple times in his life (most memorably against Mr. Tobacco Stain!). Talk about a time in your life where either you or someone else took a stand against an injustice. What were the ramifications of that event?

7. Herb and his friends certainly got themselves into some explosive shenanigans in their childhood. What was your favorite story to read about? Were you similarly mischievous as a child? Share your favorite prank story!

8. What aspects in Herb's early life helped most in developing a strong, almost to a fault, self-confidence? Who had the most influence on him—his parents or his grandparents? What aspects in your early life affected your self-confidence or the lack thereof?

9. When Herb "fell in love" with Ethelyn and had a conversation between his heart and head and ended up convincing himself not to tell her that he loved her, was he protecting Ethelyn or himself? Do you think that he did the right thing? Should he have included Ethelyn in that conversation?

10. What lessons or insights did you discover while reading *Me and the Cottonwood Tree: an Untethered Boyhood*?

11. Stop and think about the subtitle: *An Untethered Boyhood*. Was Herb given too much freedom? Do you feel that it was not freedom, but rather neglect? If you choose neglect, are you basing your choice on the first half of the twentieth century's rural norms or present-day norms? How did his freedom affect his ability to face so many moves and changes in his early life? How did it affect his ethics and personality?

ABOUT THE AUTHOR

Photo © Lifetouch

Herb Bryce was born in rural Arizona in 1933 and moved extensively throughout his childhood and teenage years. After serving four years in the Navy during the Korean War, he entered Arizona State University, where he received his undergraduate and graduate degrees. He pursued a career in the sciences and served as division chair of Physical Sciences and professor of chemistry at Citrus College and as the dean of Science and Mathematics and professor of chemistry at Seattle Central College. Herb has received the Lingafelter and Salutes to Excellence awards from the local section of the American Chemical Society. Herb admits he is left-brain dominate; however his right brain is quite active. He has a passion for the arts and is a cofounder and board member of the Shoreline–Lake Forest Park Arts Council. In his spare time he loves to travel to gain an understanding of the cultures around the world. Herb currently lives in Shoreline, Washington, where he is an active member of his local community. His philosophy is that service is the rent we pay for living. *Me and the Cottonwood Tree* is his first book. Please visit the author at www.HerbBryce.com.

CPSIA information can be obtained
at www.ICGtesting.com
Printed in the USA
LVHW092021120520
655429LV00007B/130/J